T0109951

LITERATURE

THE NEW YORK PUBLIC LIBRARY BOOK OF ANSWERS

Melinda Corey & George Ochoa

A Stonesong Press Book

A FIRESIDE BOOK

Published by Simon & Schuster
New York   London   Toronto   Sydney   Tokyo   Singapore

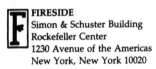 **FIRESIDE**
Simon & Schuster Building
Rockefeller Center
1230 Avenue of the Americas
New York, New York 10020

Copyright © 1993 by The New York Public Library and
The Stonesong Press, Inc.

A Stonesong Press Book

Designed by Richard Oriolo

Manufactured in the United States of America

1 3 5 7 9 10 8 6 4 2

Library of Congress Cataloging-in-Publication Data is
available.

ISBN: 0-671-78164-2

To Brother Joseph Frederick, Mrs. Geladaris,
and all our English teachers

—M.C. and G. O.

CONTENTS

CONTENTS

INTRODUCTION

I t is fitting that this third volume in *The New York Public Library Book of Answers* series is devoted to literature. After all, each of the 46 million items in the New York Public Library system represents some form of literature. In keeping with the classical definition of literature, these volumes delight and instruct. Many concentrate on instructing, whether the subject is history, science, gardening, or dog training. But many are valued mainly for their ability to delight—to please the mind, to move the heart. Such works take many forms. It may be a much-fingered copy of *Where the Wild Things Are;* the complete novels of James Michener; the plays of Shakespeare; the latest *Sports Illustrated*. In any case, the idea of literature as writing that delights is the guiding force behind *Literature: The New York Public Library Book of Answers*. Like the previous books in this series, this one is based on the kinds of questions asked by callers to The New York Public Library Telephone Reference Service (Tel-Ref). The questions cover subjects from classics to current bestsellers, from essential facts to curiosities. While one caller may ask for Goethe's full name or the five parts of "The Waste Land," another might want to know how many times Norman Mailer has been married or who was killed in *Presumed Innocent*.

To encompass this variety of questions, we have divided the book into twenty-nine categories, including the obvious (American Literature, Drama) and the more idiosyncratic (Scrapes with the Law). We have tried to cover all aspects of the life of a piece of writing, including the time and place in which it is written (The Ancient World, English Literature), its genre (Poetry, Nonfiction), the apparatus used to study it (Literary Terms, Criticism), and the writer who created it (Authors in Love, Deaths). "Literary Geography" deals with places fictitious and real, from Swift's Brobdingnag to Eudora Welty's South. "Table Talk" contains Samuel Johnson's views on writing for money and Edmund Wilson's views on Evelyn Waugh.

Like most works of writing, *Literature: The New York Public Library Book of Answers* addresses many goals, and in so doing, becomes not one thing but

INTRODUCTION

many. In this case, this seemingly simple question-and-answer book has become a curious hybrid of an English Lit survey course and a writers' edition of *People* magazine.

Over the past few decades, there have been many changes in the way we interpret literature and in the range of writers who create it. In this book, we have tried to incorporate these changes of the post-modern era, with questions on deconstructionism, logocentrism, and other important *isms* of the age, as well as on writers other than "Dead White Males"—African-Americans, Latin Americans, women, and authors who are still alive.

But, like all of the books in this series, *Literature: The New York Public Library Book of Answers* is not comprehensive. We have included more questions about areas of literature that we favor. For one thing, as two English majors, we have erred on the side of the classics. For example, there is a chapter on Shakespeare but not on Jacqueline Susann, on drama but not on movie-star biographies, more coverage of the writers of the Lost Generation than of the Brat Pack. We also made sure that our representative genres as writers are well represented. Because one of us writes essays, there is a lengthy chapter on "Nonfiction"; as another is a novelist, the "Fiction" chapter is as long. Favorite writers are well represented—Melville, Conrad, Shakespeare, Henry Adams—as well as those we love to be annoyed by—primarily Alexander Pope. We've also made sure the New York writers' contingent was mentioned, at least enough to prove that yes, it does seem that every writer lives for some time in New

York. To that end, this book answers such New York–writer questions as when Walt Whitman was the editor of the *Brooklyn Daily Eagle* and when Marianne Moore was a librarian at the New York Public Library.

Literature: The New York Public Library Book of Answers will not address the more pressing questions about modern literature—What books should remain in the canon? Will Stephen King come to write more books than Isaac Asimov? It will remind you of literary facts you once knew (How many husbands did the Wife of Bath have? Does the title *Finnegans Wake* contain an apostrophe?) or that you've often wondered about (Where did Flannery O'Connor get her peacocks? What was in that jar that Wallace Stevens placed on the hill in Tennessee?). It will also remind you of the pleasure these writers brought you. Rarely have so many authors been gathered together without a grade being given. For that reason, this book may remind you again why you read.

* * *

This book would not have been possible without the people who helped to see it to completion. To that end we thank Paul Fargis and Gail Winston for their editorial support, and Tom Brown and Greg Galloway for their editorial contributions.

MELINDA COREY AND GEORGE OCHOA

AMERICAN
LITERATURE

How was Cotton Mather related to Increase Mather?
Increase (1639–1723) was the father of Cotton (1663–1728). Both were clergymen, theologians, and prolific writers in Puritan New England.

Who is known as the "poet of the American Revolution"?
Philip Freneau (1752–1832), whose poems include "American Liberty" (1775) and "The Indian Burying Ground" (1788). He was a favorite of Thomas Jefferson's.

Where did the author of *Letters from an American Farmer* (1787) do his farming?
Michel Guillaume Jean de Crèvecoeur (1735–1813), also known as J. Hector St. John, was born in France, emigrated to Canada, and in 1759, moved to New York. He settled in Orange County, New York, where his years as a farmer led to his book. He fled back to Europe during the American Revolution.

What detective did Edgar Allan Poe invent?
C. Auguste Dupin, the coolly logical amateur sleuth of three stories published in the 1840s: "The Murders in the Rue Morgue," "The Mystery of Marie Roget," and "The Purloined Letter."

Is Poe's *The Narrative of A. Gordon Pym* (1838) based upon actual events?
Yes, the adventures of J. N. Reynolds, a stowaway who survived a mutiny, cannibalism, and other adventures.

In what work did Emerson introduce the concept of the Over-Soul?
His idea of "the soul of the whole" appeared first in the essay, "The Over-Soul," included in his *First Series* (1841).

What is the real name of the title character in *The Deerslayer* (1841)?
Nathaniel (Natty) Bumppo. In other James Fenimore Cooper novels, he is also known as Hawkeye, Leatherstocking, La Longue Carabine, and Pathfinder.

Who was Natty Bumppo's Indian sidekick?
Chingachgook. He appears in Cooper's *The Deer-slayer* (1841), *The Last of the Mohicans* (1826), *The Pathfinder* (1840), and *The Pioneers* (1823).

What is the subtitle of Nathaniel Hawthorne's *The Scarlet Letter* (1850)?
A Romance.

In the novel, who is the father of Hester Prynne's child, Pearl?
The town's minister, Arthur Dimmesdale, who is tormented by his illicit act.

Which came first, *Omoo* or *Typee*?
Melville's novels of the South Seas were published in this order: *Typee* in 1846, *Omoo* in 1847.

Who are Captain Ahab's mates in Melville's *Moby-Dick* (1851)?
The first mate is Starbuck, the second is Stubb, the third is Flask.

Who are Ahab's harpooneers?
Queequeg, Tashtego, and Daggoo.

Who was Mocha Dick?
A legendary white whale said to have killed more than thirty men and attacked several ships in the 1800s. His story was told in *The Knickerbocker Magazine* in 1839. Melville's *Moby-Dick* of 1851 may have been influenced by the story.

What is the repeated response of Bartleby the Scrivener to his boss?
Melville's model of passive resistance calmly replies, "I would prefer not to." The short story "Bartleby the Scrivener" was first published anonymously in *Putnam's Magazine* in 1853.

What is a scrivener?
A copier of legal documents.

When did Thoreau live in his hut at Walden Pond?
For two years from 1845 to 1847. His account of the experience, *Walden, or Life in the Woods,* appeared in 1854.

How well was Walt Whitman's *Leaves of Grass* initially received?
It is estimated that the first edition of one of the great American poems sold no more than three dozen copies when it was first published in 1855.

What was the name of "The Celebrated Jumping Frog of Calaveras County"?
The animal in the 1865 Mark Twain story is named Dan'l Webster.

What does the "T" in Booker T. Washington (1856–1915) stand for?
He was born Booker Taliaferro. He adopted the name "Washington" during his school years. His works include the autobiography *Up from Slavery* (1901).

What year was Stephen Crane born?
The author of *The Red Badge of Courage* (1895) was born in 1871, six years after the end of the Civil War. He died in 1900.

What was Kate Chopin's ethnic heritage?
She was born Kate O'Flaherty (1851–1904) in St. Louis, Missouri, to an Irish father and French mother. Her married name came from her husband, Oscar Chopin. Her fiction includes the novel *The Awakening* (1899).

What is the octopus in *The Octopus* (1901)?
The octopus in Frank Norris's novel is the Pacific and Southwestern Railroad, which dominates the California state government, manipulates other industries, and oppresses struggling wheat farmers.

What is the name of the stockyard district where main character Jurgis Rudkis lives and works in *The Jungle*?
It is known as Packingtown, in Chicago. The 1906 book led to the passage of the Pure Food and Drug Act.

What is the source of O. Henry's title *The Four Million* (1906)?
The title of O. Henry's short story collection refers to two things: it represents the population of New York City at the time, and it is an answer to Ward McAllister, who said "there are only about 400 people in

New York society." The collection contains the 1902 story, "The Gift of the Magi."

What kind of an accident cripples Ethan Frome in Edith Wharton's novel, *Ethan Frome* (1911)?
He and his beloved, Mattie Silver, drive a sled into a tree in a botched suicide attempt.

What was Ernest Hemingway's first published book?
His first book was *Three Stories and Ten Poems* (1923); it was published in France in a small edition. His first book published in the United States was *In Our Time* (1925), an expanded edition of the version published in France in 1924.

How many stories comprise Sherwood Anderson's *Winesburg, Ohio* (1919)?
Twenty-three.

Where was Jay Gatsby supposed to have gone to school?
Oxford. In Fitzgerald's *The Great Gatsby* (1925) the gangster Wolfsheim said Gatsby was an "Oggsford" man.

What is the source of the title of Thomas Wolfe's novel *Look Homeward, Angel* (1929)?
John Milton's poem "Lycidas" (1637). Milton asks his dead friend, now an angel, to look back compassionately on his still-living friends:

> Look homeward, Angel, now, and melt with ruth:
> And, O ye dolphins, waft the hapless youth.

How old is Benjy in Faulkner's novel *The Sound and the Fury* (1929)?
The retarded narrator of the first section of the novel is thirty-three years old. Faulkner asked that Benjy's stream of consciousness be printed in eight different colors of type to better express the layers of Benjy's memory. The request was not granted.

Who were the Fugitives and Agrarians?
A group of writers associated with Vanderbilt University in Nashville in the 1920s and 1930s. The most famous of the group were Robert Penn Warren, John Crowe Ransom, Allen Tate, and Donald Davidson.

What are the books in John Dos Passos's *U.S.A.* trilogy?
They are:
  The 42nd Parallel (1930)
  1919 (1932)
  The Big Money (1936)
The three were first published together in 1937.

What works comprise *Pale Horse, Pale Rider*?
There are three short novels in the 1939 collection by Katherine Anne Porter:
  1. "Pale Horse, Pale Rider"
  2. "Noon Wine"
  3. "Old Mortality"

Who is the hero of William Faulkner's *Light in August* (1932)?
Joe Christmas, a man believed to be part black, who murders a white woman named Joanna Burden and is castrated and killed for it.

Who is the hero of Richard Wright's *Native Son* (1940)?
Bigger Thomas, a black man from Chicago who murders a white woman and is executed for it.

Who is the hero of Ralph Ellison's *Invisible Man* (1952)?
He has no name. He is a young man from the South who finds his way to a hidden existence in a coal cellar in New York.

What is the source of the title of Richard Wright's *Native Son* (1940)?
Wright took the title from Nelson Algren, after the title was rejected for Algren's novel *Somebody in Boots* (1935).

What paper did Miss Lonelyhearts write for?
The male advice columnist wrote for the *New York Post-Dispatch* in Nathanael West's *Miss Lonelyhearts* (1946).

> **What was his real name?**
> It was never given.

What church did Hazel Motes found in Flannery O'Connor's *Wise Blood* (1952)?
He founded the Church Without Christ, "where the blind don't see and the lame don't walk and what's dead stays that way." A charlatan named Onnie Jay Holy started a rival sect, the Holy Church of Christ Without Christ.

What is the rest of the nursery rhyme from which Ken Kesey took the title for his novel *One Flew Over the Cuckoo's Nest* (1962)?
Wire, briar, limber, lock,
Three geese in a flock,
One flew East, one flew West,
One flew over the cuckoo's nest.

Did Alice Walker start out by writing fiction or poetry?
The first published work of the poet and novelist was a book of poetry: *Once: Poems* (1968). She followed up soon after, however, with a novel: *The Third Life of Grange Copeland* (1970).

How many Rabbit novels has John Updike written?
Four: *Rabbit Run* (1960), *Rabbit Redux* (1971), *Rabbit Is Rich* (1981), and *Rabbit at Rest* (1990). The hero of all four is Harry Angstrom, nicknamed "Rabbit."

What is the rainbow in Thomas Pynchon's *Gravity's Rainbow* (1973)?
The arc a rocket makes from launch to target. The novel is set in World War II Europe at the time German V-2 rockets were falling on London.

Who was the model for Saul Bellow's hard-drinking poet Von Humboldt Fleisher in his novel *Humboldt's Gift* (1975)?
Bellow's friend Delmore Schwartz (1913–66), poet, fiction writer, and critic.

Where is the house in *Housekeeping*?
The 1981 novel by Marilynne Robinson is set in Fingerbone, Montana.

How long is the time span covered in *The Mezzanine* (1988)?
The novel by Nicholson Baker tells the story of a single lunch hour. Much of the book focuses on an escalator ride.

What is the connection between William Kennedy's novel *Quinn's Book* (1988) and his Albany Cycle?
Albany-born Daniel Quinn, the protagonist of *Quinn's Book*, is the grandfather of Danny Quinn of *Ironweed* (1983). *Ironweed* is part of the Albany Cycle, which also includes *Legs* (1975), *Billy Phelan's Greatest Game* (1978), and *Very Old Bones* (1992).

What new Hemingway novel was published in the 1980s?
The Garden of Eden, published posthumously by Scribners in 1986.

THE ANCIENT WORLD

How old is *The Epic of Gilgamesh*?
The Babylonian epic dates back to about 2000 B.C. It concerns the adventures of the hero Gilgamesh and the "wild man" Enkidu, and Gilgamesh's grief over Enkidu's death.

What sets off the quarrel between Achilles and Agamemnon at the beginning of Homer's *The Iliad* (ninth century B.C.)?
Agamemnon, commander-in-chief of the Greek armies at Troy, is forced to return a captive woman named Chryseis in order to stop a pestilence sent by

the god Apollo. Agamemnon demands Achilles' captive Briseis in exchange. Achilles, in anger, refuses to fight for the Greeks any longer.

In what language was the Bible originally written?
The Old Testament was written in Hebrew; it dates from the thirteenth to the first century B.C. The New Testament was written in Greek in the first century A.D.

How did the monsters Scylla and Charybdis wreak havoc?
Scylla, a female six-headed monster, captured sailors and ate them. Charybdis was a whirlpool (or a creator of whirlpools) that swallowed ships. The two creatures lay in wait on either side of the Straits of Messina between Italy and Sicily. Their story is told in Homer's *Odyssey* (ninth century B.C.).

What are the books of the Pentateuch?
They are the first five books of the Hebrew Bible or Old Testament: Genesis, Exodus, Leviticus, Numbers, and Deuteronomy. Named from Greek *penta* (five) and *teuchos* (book), tradition assigned their authorship to Moses.

In what book of Homer's *Iliad* (ninth century B.C.) does the "Catalogue of Ships" appear?
The Greek ships are enumerated in Book II.

In what book of Homer's *Odyssey* (ninth century B.C.) does Odysseus descend into the underworld?
Book XI of XXIV.

In what book of Vergil's *Aeneid* (19 B.C.) does Aeneas descend into the underworld?
Book VI of XII.

How many Homeric hymns survive?
Thirty-three of these poems in honor of various Greek gods survive. Written in imitation of Homer, they date from the eighth century B.C. to the fifth or fourth century B.C.

What did Hesiod do for a living?
The reputed author of the *Theogony*, the oldest surviving account of the origin of the Greek gods, was a poor Boeotian farmer of the eighth century B.C. His *Works and Days* gives advice on farming and moral life.

Whom did some classical writers call the "tenth muse"?
Sappho (b. 612 B.C.), a lyric poet whose work exists only in fragments. Married, she lived in Lesbos and led a group of women who were devoted to music and poetry.

Who were Shadrach, Meshach, and Abednego?
They were three Jews who were thrown into a fiery furnace by order of King Nebuchadnezzar in chapter 3 of the Old Testament Book of Daniel, as punishment for refusing to worship a golden idol. God saved them, however, allowing them to walk through the fire unharmed.

What classical writer was the first to record the story about the runner who ran from Marathon to Athens, and then died?
It was Lucian of Samosata, a writer of satirical essays of the second century A.D. Where he got the story is unknown. He claimed that Philippides (also known as Pheidippides) ran about twenty-five miles from the battlefield of Marathon to Athens to bring news of the Greek victory over Persia, in September 490 B.C.

What are the names of the three tragedies in Aeschylus's *Oresteia*?
Agamemnon, The Libation Bearers, and *The Eumenides,* all first presented in 458 B.C.

What is the riddle of the Sphinx?
"What animal walks on four legs in the morning, two at noon, and three at night?" the Sphinx asks Oedipus, the hero of Sophocles' play *Oedipus Rex* (426 B.C.). Oedipus answers that it is man (crawling as an infant, walking erect as an adult, and walking with a staff in old age).

Who are the two brothers of Antigone? Which one does she bury against King Creon's will in Sophocles' *Antigone* (441 B.C.)?
Her two brothers are Eteocles and Polyneices. Both are dead when the play opens, but Creon forbids the burial of Polyneices, who had rebelled against Creon's rule. Antigone gives him a token burial anyway. Antigone also has a sister, Ismene.

What was Medea's heritage?
She was the Princess of Colchis and the wife of Jason, the King of Iolcus. Her father was King Aeetes of Colchis. *Medea*, by Euripides, was first performed in 431 B.C.

What war were women protesting in Aristophanes' comedy, *Lysistrata* (c. 415 B.C.)?
The Peloponnesian War between Athens and Sparta, waged from 431 to 404 B.C. In the play, the women of Athens and Sparta refuse to have sex with their husbands until peace is made.

What was the name of Socrates' wife?
Famed for her shrewishness, the wife of the fifth-century B.C. Athenian philosopher was named Xantippe.

What epic features Laocoön?
The Trojan priest who was killed by sea serpents is a character in Vergil's *Aeneid* (c. 19 B.C.).

How large were the Augean Stables that Hercules had to clean?
The stables held 3,000 cattle and had not been cleaned in thirty years. Cleaning them was the sixth of Hercules' seven labors. Hercules' story was told by Ovid (43 B.C.–17 A.D.) and Apollodorus (first–second century A.D.).

Were Homer's works ever banned?
Yes. Roman emperor Caligula banned them during

his reign (37–41 A.D.) because they were said to promote unhealthy ideas about Greek freedom.

Which New Testament Gospel was written first?
It is generally accepted that the Gospel of Mark was written before those of Matthew, Luke, and John. The New Testament places them in the order Matthew, Mark, Luke, and John.

What does "Q" mean to Biblical scholars?
It is the hypothetical source used by synoptic evangelists Matthew and Luke. Never found, it is believed to contain the sayings and stories that Matthew and Luke, but not Mark, share. The term comes from German *Quelle*, or "source."

Where in the Bible does the "Whore of Babylon" appear?
In the New Testament Book of Revelation 17:1–7. The whore sits on a scarlet beast with seven heads and ten horns. She holds a cup of abominations and has written on her forehead: "Babylon the Great, the Mother of Harlots and Abominations of the Earth." She was probably meant originally to represent the Roman Empire.

Who is featured in Plutarch's *Lives*?
The *Parallel Lives* (first century A.D.) pairs biographies of famous Greeks and Romans, such as the orators Demosthenes and Cicero. The book provided background for some of Shakespeare's plays, including *Julius Caesar*.

What classical writer told the story of Jason and the Argonauts?

The most complete treatment is the *Argonautica* by third-century poet Apollonius of Rhodes.

Where did the Argonauts get their name?

They were the crew of the ship *Argo*, which sailed in quest of the Golden Fleece.

What is a "cento"?

From the Latin for "patchwork," a cento is a poem or other literary work composed of lines or passages from other, more famous works, with the meaning altered. Centos were a favorite form in late antiquity. An example is the *Cento Vergilianus* by Proba Falconia (fourth century), which used bits of Vergil to recount sacred history.

When did the Vulgate Bible first appear?

The Latin translation of the Bible was written mostly by St. Jerome in 382–384 A.D. The term comes from Latin *editio vulgata*, "spread among the people."

AUTHORS IN LOVE

Who was older, Beatrice or Dante?
Born in 1266, Beatrice Portinari, wife of Simone de' Bardi, was Dante's junior by one year. They were in their youth when Dante (1265–1321) fell in love with her. She died in 1290, leaving Dante in mourning. He wrote about her in the *Vita Nuova* (1294) and the *Divine Comedy* (1321).

How many years of age separated Shakespeare and his wife?
She was eight years older. They were married in 1582, when he was eighteen.

31

Whom did Jonathan Swift call "Stella"?
"Stella" was Esther Johnson, a woman Swift once tutored at the household of Sir William Temple in England. Swift's letters to Johnson and her companion Rebecca Dingley, written from 1710 to 1713, are known as *Journal to Stella*.

What became of Percy Shelley's first wife?
Harriet Westbrook Shelley committed suicide by drowning in 1816, two years after Shelley left her for Mary Wollstonecraft. Shelley had eloped with the sixteen-year-old Harriet in 1811. Shelley himself died by drowning in a boating accident aboard his schooner, *Ariel*, in 1822.

When did Washington Irving (1783–1859) court Mary Shelley (1797–1851)?
Irving and fellow American writer John H. Payne were said to have competed for the affection of the author of *Frankenstein* during a visit to France from 1824 to 1826. Mary's husband Percy Shelley had died two years earlier.

Why did Robert Browning (1812–89) and Elizabeth Barrett (1806–61) have to marry secretly?
Because Barrett's father refused to let his children marry—even though Elizabeth was forty at the time. The secret wedding took place at London's St. Marylebone Church on September 12, 1846. (Browning was thirty-four.) They lived in Florence for fifteen happy years until her death in 1861.

AUTHORS IN LOVE

Who divorced English art critic John Ruskin (1819–1900) on grounds of impotence?

Euphemia Chalmers ("Effie") Gray. Gray obtained an annulment in 1854 after seven years of an unconsummated marriage. She went on to marry painter John Everett Millais, a favorite of Ruskin's.

Who was George Eliot's (1819–80) living companion?

Writer George Henry Lewes (1817–78), who was officially married to another woman, Agnes, but unable to get a divorce. Eliot and Lewes lived together from 1854 until his death in 1878.

Whom did Maud Gonne (1866–1953) marry?

Not William Butler Yeats, the poet who made the actress famous through his poems of unrequited love. In 1903, after knowing Yeats for fourteen years, Gonne married Major John MacBride, an Irish revolutionary characterized by Yeats as a "drunken, vainglorious lout." MacBride was executed for his role in the Easter Rebellion against the British in 1916. In 1917, Yeats gave up waiting for Gonne and married Georgie Hyde Lees.

How long did Edith Wharton's marriage last?

New York socialite Edith Newbold Jones (1862–1937) married George Wharton in 1885. Their marriage lasted twenty-seven years until 1912, when she divorced him. By then she was living in France, where she remained until her death.

How many years of age separated Will and Ariel Durant?
Twelve. The authors of the multivolume series *The Story of Civilization* (1935–67) were married in New York City in 1913, when he was twenty-seven and she was fifteen.

How long was novelist and critic Rebecca West (1892–1983) the lover of H. G. Wells?
After her review of Wells's book, *Marriage*, in 1912, they met and began their ten-year relationship. Their son, Anthony West, born in 1914, became a novelist and critic in his own right.

On what day did James Joyce (1882–1941) and his future wife, Nora Barnacle, have their first date?
Probably June 16, 1904—Bloomsday, the day on which *Ulysses* (1922) is set. She was then a chambermaid at Finn's Hotel, Dublin.

When did James Joyce get married?
Joyce married Nora Barnacle in 1931, just ten years before his death. They had lived together since 1904.

What hotel threw out newlyweds F. Scott Fitzgerald and Zelda Sayre?
The Biltmore Hotel in New York City, following their wedding on April 3, 1920. The management asked them to leave because of their unseemly behavior.

AUTHORS IN LOVE

When did critic and writer C. S. Lewis marry Joy Davidman?
In 1956. She died of cancer in 1960, three years before Lewis's own death in 1963. Their story is told in Lewis's *A Grief Observed* (1961).

How many times was Ernest Hemingway married?
Four.

How many times was Henry Miller married?
Four.

How many times has Norman Mailer been married?
Six.

AWARDS

Who was the first woman to be awarded the Nobel Prize in Literature?
Selma Lagerlöf of Sweden was awarded the prize in 1909. She is known for such works as *Jerusalem* (1901–02), a collection of stories about Swedish peasant life.

Who was the first African-American to win the Pulitzer Prize in Literature?
Gwendolyn Brooks in 1950, for *Annie Allen*.

What novel won the first Pulitzer Prize?
His Family by Ernest Poole in 1918.

What play?
Why Marry? by Jesse L. Williams in 1918.

How many Pulitzer prizes did Eugene O'Neill win?
Four, for *Beyond the Horizon* (1920), *Anna Christie* (1922), *Strange Interlude* (1928), and *Long Day's Journey into Night* (1957).

How many did Robert Frost win?
Four, for *New Hampshire* (1924), *Collected Poems* (1931), *A Further Range* (1937), and *A Witness Tree* (1943).

How many did Ernest Hemingway win?
One, for *The Old Man and the Sea* (1952).

What works earned Edith Wharton her Pulitzer prizes?
The first woman to receive the award twice, Wharton was awarded the Pulitzer in Literature in 1920 for *The Age of Innocence* and in Drama in 1935 for *The Old Maid*.

Who is the Newbery behind the Newbery Medal?
John Newbery (1713–67) of England was one of the first publishers to publish books for children. The Newbery Medal, established in his name in 1921, is awarded each year for the best American children's book.

Who received the first Newbery Medal?
The American Library Association awarded the first Newbery in 1922 to Hendrik Willem Van Loon for *The Story of Mankind* (1921).

Who received the first Caldecott Medal?
The illustrator's counterpart to the Newbery Medal, named for English illustrator Randolph Caldecott, was first awarded in 1938 to Dorothy P. Lathrop for *Animals of the Bible*.

Which American writers have been awarded the Nobel Prize in Literature?
Ten Americans have been awarded the prize: Sinclair Lewis (1930); Eugene O'Neill (1936); Pearl S. Buck (1938); William Faulkner (1949); Ernest Hemingway (1954); John Steinbeck (1962); Saul Bellow (1976); Isaac Bashevis Singer, a naturalized citizen (1978); Czeslaw Milosz, a naturalized citizen (1980); and Joseph Brodsky, a naturalized citizen (1987).

Who has been awarded the O. Henry Prize for short stories more times than any other writer?
The Society of Arts and Sciences gave the prize three times to Stephen Vincent Benét—for "An End to Dreams" (1932), "The Devil and Daniel Webster" (1937), and "Freedom's a Hard-Bought Thing" (1940). Benét was also awarded the Pulitzer Prize in poetry for *John Brown's Body* in 1929.

Who was the first winner of the Bollingen Prize?
The annual prize for poetry was first awarded in 1949 to Ezra Pound for his *Pisan Cantos* (1948).

Who received the first National Book Award for Fiction?
Nelson Algren in 1950 for *The Man with the Golden Arm*.

When and for what work did Winston Churchill win the Nobel Prize in Literature?
In 1953 for *The Second World War.*

When was the Pulitzer Prize for general nonfiction established?
It was first awarded in 1962 to Theodore H. White for *The Making of the President 1960.*

Who was awarded the Pulitzer Prize in Fiction in 1973?
Judges and trustees were divided so sharply over Thomas Pynchon's novel *Gravity's Rainbow* that for only the seventh time in Pulitzer history no award was given.

In what year did Jean-Paul Sartre refuse the Nobel Prize in Literature?
In 1964. He explained: "A writer must refuse to allow himself to be transformed into an institution."

CHARACTERS

In the Bible, who are Ishmael's parents?
According to the Book of Genesis, Ishmael is the son of Abraham and Hagar.

In *The Iliad* (ninth century B.C.), what goddess is Achilles' mother?
Thetis, a sea nymph.

> **What god is Helen's father?**
> Zeus.

> **What goddess is Aeneas's mother?**
> Venus.

What gods are Hector's parents?
None. His parents, Priam and Hecuba, are both human.

What did Judas receive for betraying Christ?
Thirty pieces of silver. In Matthew's Gospel, Judas throws away the money and hangs himself after the betrayal.

What is the connection between Roland and Orlando?
They are the same character. Roland, knight of Charlemagne's court, is the hero of *The Song of Roland*, an eleventh-century French epic. Orlando is the Italian form of Roland's name; he appears in Ariosto's *Orlando Furioso* (1532).

Where in literature did Merlin the sorcerer first appear?
In Geoffrey of Monmouth's *The History of the Kings of Britain* (1137). This Latin prose work by the English chronicler also helped build the legend of Merlin's protégé, King Arthur.

Who is Scheherazade?
She is the narrator of the *Arabian Nights* (c. 1450), who tells stories night after night to keep her husband, the Sultan Schahriah, from strangling her at dawn. Scheherazade tells her stories to her sister Dinarzade in the Sultan's hearing.

What was the name of the Faerie Queene in Spenser's *The Faerie Queene* (1590–96)?
Gloriana.

What happens to Faust at the end of Christopher Marlowe's *Dr. Faustus* (1588)?
The scholar who sells his soul to Satan is torn apart by devils.

> **What happens to him at the end of Goethe's *Faust* (1808)?**
> His soul is rescued by a choir of angels.

How old is Juliet in *Romeo and Juliet* (c. 1596)?
In act 1, scene 2, her father says she "hath not seen the change of fourteen years"—making her thirteen.

Who is the referee in the duel between Hamlet and Laertes in Act 5 of Shakespeare's *Hamlet* (c. 1601)?
Osric, a foppish courtier.

What was the name of Don Quixote's horse?
Rocinante. The scrawny old horse and its rider appeared in Cervantes's *Don Quixote de la Mancha* (1605, 1615).

Was there a real Robinson Crusoe?
Daniel Defoe based *The Life and Strange Adventures of Robinson Crusoe* (1719–20) on the real-life story of Alexander Selkirk (1676–1721), a Scottish sailor who survived for more than four years on the desert island of Juan Fernandez off the Chilean coast. He be-

came a celebrity after his rescue and homecoming in 1709.

Who was Martinus Scriblerus?
The pseudonym was adopted by several members of the Scriblerus Club, a group formed to ridicule "false tastes in learning." Members of the club included Jonathan Swift, John Arbuthnot, Alexander Pope, and John Gay. The *Memoirs of Martinus Scriblerus*, written mainly by Arbuthnot, were issued in 1741.

Who lived in the Castle of Otranto?
It was inhabited by Manfred, the Prince of Otranto, with his family, in the 1764 Gothic novel *The Castle of Otranto* by Horace Walpole.

Was there a real Baron Münchausen?
Yes. Baron Karl Friedrich Hieronymus von Münchausen (1720-1797), a German adventurer, is believed to have served in the Russian army against the Turks. He was known for exaggerating his exploits. Satirical stories about him were told by Rodolf Erich Raspe in *Baron Münchausen, Narrative of his Marvellous Travels* (1785).

What is the name of the title character in *The Monk*?
Father Ambrosio, of Madrid. He kills two women who turn out to be his mother, Elvira, and his sister, Antonia, in the 1795 novel by Matthew Lewis.

What happened to Ichabod Crane?
At the end of *The Legend of Sleepy Hollow* (1819), Wash-

ington Irving's schoolmaster disappears after being hit by the Headless Horseman's "head."

Who is the speaker in Robert Browning's "My Last Duchess" (1842)?
Alfonso II, the Duke of Ferrara in the mid-sixteenth century.

Who is "Childe Roland" and what does he do at the Dark Tower?
In Robert Browning's poem, "Childe Roland to the Dark Tower Came" (1855), Childe Roland is a knight errant in search of the Dark Tower; when he reaches it he blows his horn, and the poem ends. The title comes from a piece of a song in Shakespeare's *King Lear* (act 3, scene 4).

Which character spontaneously combusts in Charles Dickens's *Bleak House* (1852)?
Krook, the junk merchant.

Was there a real Mr. Micawber?
Wilkins Micawber, the schemer in *David Copperfield* (1861), is said to be based on Charles Dickens's own father.

Who was Simon Legree and where did he come from?
The archetypal villain first appeared in Harriet Beecher Stowe's *Uncle Tom's Cabin* (1852) as the brutal degenerate who flogs Tom to death.

CHARACTERS

What is the name of Isabel Archer's stepdaughter in Henry James's *The Portrait of a Lady* (1881)?
Pansy. Her father, Isabel's husband, is Gilbert Osmond; her mother is Madame Merle.

Who was first called "Pooh-Bah"?
The Lord High Everything in W. S. Gilbert and Arthur Sullivan's operetta *The Mikado* (1885).

What are Jekyll's and Hyde's first names?
In the 1886 work by Robert Louis Stevenson, *The Strange Case of Dr. Jekyll and Mr. Hyde,* Henry Jekyll is the London doctor who creates the potion that turns him into Edward Hyde.

What was Mr. Dooley's first name?
Martin. The Irish saloon keeper was created by Chicago newspaperman Finley Peter Dunne in 1892, and provided the moniker for a series of satirical books by Dunne, including *Mr. Dooley in Peace and in War* (1898) and *Mr. Dooley's Opinions* (1901).

In Rudyard Kipling's *Kim* (1901), what is Kim's full name?
Kimball O'Hara.

What are the special powers of Rima the Bird Girl?
In *Green Mansions* (1904) by William H. Hudson, Rima the Bird Girl is able to understand the language spoken by the creatures who live in the South American forests.

What is the name of the playboy in J. M. Synge's
***The Playboy of the Western World* (1907)?**
Christy Mahon, a young fugitive who thinks he has
killed his domineering father and is therefore lionized
by villagers—especially women.

Who was the "Glad Girl"?
Pollyanna, in the eponymous 1913 novel by Eleanor
Hodgman Porter. She also appeared in the 1915 se-
quel, *Pollyanna Grows Up*.

Who was Jeeves's boss?
Bertie Wooster, a young man-about-town in P. G.
Wodehouse's stories beginning with *My Man Jeeves*
(1919). Jeeves was his valet.

**What artist's life is the basis for W. Somerset
Maugham's novel *The Moon and Sixpence* (1919)?**
Paul Gauguin's. In the novel, Charles Strickland is a
London stockbroker who leaves his family to paint in
the South Seas.

What is Babbitt's profession?
George F. Babbitt, the lead character in Sinclair
Lewis's *Babbitt* (1922), is a real-estate dealer in Zenith,
an average American city. He is married to Myra Babbitt; his children are named Verona and Ted.

**In what Hemingway short story does Nick Adams
first appear?**
Hemingway's alter ego, the central figure of *In Our
Time* (1924), makes his first appearance in "Indian
Camp" (1923).

What is Mrs. Dalloway's first name?
The title character of the 1925 novel by Virginia Woolf is named Clarissa.

What is the name of the lover in D. H. Lawrence's *Lady Chatterley's Lover* (1928)?
Oliver Mellors, gamekeeper for Lady Chatterley's husband.

What was the name of the daughter of Rhett Butler and Scarlett O'Hara in Margaret Mitchell's *Gone With the Wind* (1936)?
Bonnie Blue Butler. She is killed at an early age in a riding accident.

Who is the central figure in James Joyce's *Finnegans Wake* (1939)?
The main character is Humphrey Chimpden Earwicker, a pubkeeper in Dublin who is trying to live down an undisclosed crime he committed against a young woman (or man) in the park. Earwicker is also known as Here Comes Everybody and Haveth Childer Everywhere, and is linked with Adam, Jesus Christ, Napoleon, Jonathan Swift, and Tristram.

In Hemingway's *The Old Man and the Sea* (1952), what fish does Santiago catch?
A marlin.

What was the name of Holden Caulfield's roommate in *The Catcher in the Rye* (1951)?
Stradlater was the rich and conceited roommate.

What Kurt Vonnegut character invented ice-nine?
Dr. Felix Hoenikker in *Cat's Cradle* (1963). Ice-nine is
a form of water that freezes at 114.4 degrees Fahren-
heit. When it is accidentally released into the ocean, it
freezes the entire world.

**Who is the psychiatrist to whom Alexander Portnoy
tells his story in Philip Roth's *Portnoy's Complaint*
(1969)?**
Dr. Spielvogel.

CHILDREN'S
LITERATURE

Who was Mother Goose?
She first appeared in Charles Perrault's *Mother Goose Tales* (1697), a collection of popular folk stories. She is depicted at the front of the book in an illustration of an old woman telling tales by firelight to children.

What happens to Little Red Riding Hood?
In Charles Perrault's original version (1697), the wolf devours the "prettiest girl that ever was seen." In the Brothers Grimm version (1812), called "Little Red Cap," a hunter cuts open the wolf with a pair of scissors and frees the girl and her grandmother.

What were Cinderella's slippers made of?
Charles Perrault's 1697 French version of the tale has Cinderella wearing glass (*verre*) slippers, but his sources gave her fur (*vair*) slippers. Perrault's alteration may have been accidental.

What were the names of the Brothers Grimm?
Jacob Ludwig and Wilhelm Carl.

Which was younger?
Wilhelm Carl (1786-1859; Jacob, 1785-1863). Their book *Children's and Household Tales*, now known as *Grimm's Fairy-Tales*, first appeared in 1812.

What was Hans Christian Andersen's first published work?
His novel *The Improvisatore* was published in 1835. Later the same year, Andersen published *Tales Told for Children*, which included well-known tales as well as an original story, "Little Ida's Flowers."

Who did Jo March marry in *Little Women* (1868-69)?
An elderly German professor named Mr. Bhaer.

Who wrote *Tom Brown's School Days* (1857)?
Thomas Hughes, English jurist. The book for boys tells of young Tom Brown's adventures at Rugby. Hughes also wrote a sequel, *Tom Brown at Oxford* (1861).

Who was the model for Alice in Lewis Carroll's *Alice's Adventures in Wonderland* (1865)?
Alice Liddell, daughter of Henry George Liddell, Dean of Christ Church, Oxford.

Who wins the silver skates in *Hans Brinker*?
It is not Hans Brinker, but his sister Gretel, according to the 1865 novel by Mary Mapes Dodge.

Who wrote the Uncle Remus stories?
Joel Chandler Harris adapted the folktales, which were first published in the Atlanta *Constitution* and were later collected in *Uncle Remus, His Songs and His Sayings* (1880).

Who wrote *The Adventures of Pinocchio* (1883)?
Italian author Carlo Collodi (a.k.a. Carlo Lorenzini) wrote the popular tale of a puppet who comes to life.

Who invented the golliwog?
The golliwog, a type of doll known as "the blackest gnome," was invented by Florence K. Upton in *The Adventures of Two Dutch Dolls and a "Golliwog"* (1895). More golliwog tales followed until 1909.

What were the names of the Bobbsey Twins?
There were two sets of twins: Bert and Nan and their younger siblings, Freddie and Flossie. The series about them began with *The Bobbsey Twins* (1904) by Laura Lee Hope.

Who created the Bobbsey Twins?
New Jersey novelist Edward Stratemeyer, under the pseudonym Laura Lee Hope.

Who created Tom Swift?
Stratemeyer, under the pseudonym Victor Appleton.

Who created the Hardy Boys?
Stratemeyer again, under the pseudonym Franklin W. Dixon.

Who created Nancy Drew?
Stratemeyer, under the pseudonym Carolyn Keene. The prolific author died in 1930.

In James M. Barrie's play *Peter Pan* (1904), how did Captain Hook lose his hand?
A crocodile ate it, then followed him around the seas in search of more of him.

What does the A.A. in A. A. Milne stand for?
Alan Alexander. Milne is best known as the author of *Winnie-the-Pooh* (1926) and *The House at Pooh Corner* (1928).

What does the E.H. in E. H. Shepard stand for?
Ernest Howard. Shepard illustrated A. A. Milne's *Winnie-the-Pooh* books (1926-28) and the 1931 edition of Kenneth Grahame's *The Wind in the Willows* (1908).

What was Felix Salten's real name?
Siegmund Salzmann. Under the pen name "Salten," the German author wrote *Bambi* (1923). The first English translation was published in 1928.

Who invented Mary Poppins?
P. L. Travers, in a series of books beginning with *Mary Poppins* in 1934.

What was the first book published by Dr. Seuss (Theodor Geisel)?
And to Think I Saw It on Mulberry Street was published in 1937 by Vanguard Press, after being rejected by twenty-three other publishers.

Who created Babar the Elephant?
Jean de Brunhoff, in stories beginning with *The Story of Babar* (1933). De Brunhoff's son Laurent continued the series.

Whose friend is *My Friend Flicka* (1941)?
In the novel by Mary O'Hara, Flicka, a half-wild filly, is the friend of ten-year-old Ken McLaughlin in Wyoming.

What are the books of *The Chronicles of Narnia*?
The series of seven children's books by C. S. Lewis started in 1950 with *The Lion, the Witch, and the Wardrobe*, and continued with *Prince Caspian, The Voyage of the Dawn Treader, The Silver Chair, The Magician's Nephew, The Horse and His Boy*, and *The Last Battle*.

What was the first message woven into Charlotte's web?
In the 1952 novel *Charlotte's Web* by E. B. White, the first message Charlotte the spider writes in her web is "SOME PIG!"

In William Golding's *Lord of the Flies* (1954), who is the sadistic leader of the hunters?
Jack.

Who is the overweight bespectacled boy?
Piggy.

Who is the embattled elected leader?
Ralph.

What was Maurice Sendak's first book?
The author/illustrator was a designer of window displays in a toy store when he was commissioned to illustrate *The Wonderful Farm* by Marcel Aymé in 1951. Sendak wrote and illustrated his first children's book, *Kenny's Window*, in 1956.

Who wrote *One Hundred and One Dalmatians*?
The source of the popular Disney film was Dodie Smith's 1956 novel.

Which teenager dies in John Knowles's *A Separate Peace* (1959)?
Phineas. Gene, the novel's narrator, survives to tell the tale. The two are students at the Devon School in New Hampshire during World War II.

What is the name of the little boy who goes to the country of the Wild Things in Maurice Sendak's *Where the Wild Things Are* (1963)?
Max.

Does the title character in Eric Carle's *The Very Hungry Caterpillar* (1969) have a name?
No.

What was Judy Blume's first book?
Are You There God? It's Me, Margaret, published in 1970.

What book by Dr. Seuss has sold the most copies?
Green Eggs and Ham, published in 1960, has sold over 6 million copies. Another 1960 book, *One Fish, Two Fish, Red Fish, Blue Fish*, has sold nearly as many.

When did Dr. Seuss die?
Theodor Seuss Geisel died on September 24, 1991, at age eighty-seven. Dr. Seuss had written about fifty books that sold more than 200 million copies. His last book, *Oh, the Places You'll Go* (1990), was still on the bestseller list when he died.

COMPARATIVE LITERATURE

When was the Koran written?
It existed first in oral form as a series of revelations recited by the prophet Muhammad (570–632), founder
of Islam. His followers wrote down or committed to
memory the individual surahs, or chapters, but these
were not collected in authoritative form until about
650.

How old is *The Tale of Genji*?
This Japanese novel was written by court lady
Murasaki Shikibu around 1000. It was first translated

into English by Arthur Waley in 1925–33. It is widely thought of as the world's first novel.

What is the highest of Dante's heavens?
In the *Paradiso* (1321), it is the Empyrean, the tenth heaven. It contains God's Court, seen as a many-petaled rose.

What does the title of Boccaccio's *The Decameron* (1350–52) mean?
It means "ten days" and refers to the number of days the narrators spend telling stories. One hundred stories are told by seven women and three men during the Black Death of 1348.

Why was the hero of *Orlando Furioso* furious?
In the Italian poem by Ariosto (1532), the knight Orlando goes crazy with rage when he learns that Angelica, the woman he loves, has married someone else. Orlando runs around naked, destroying everything in sight. By the poem's end, he is cured.

How are Gargantua and Pantagruel related?
In Rabelais's French satire *Gargantua and Pantagruel* (1533), Gargantua is Pantagruel's father. Both are giants who go on humorous adventures.

Which crusade is the subject of *Jerusalem Delivered*?
The Italian religious epic, written in 1575 by Torquato Tasso (1544–95), concerns the First Crusade, in which European Christians fought to regain the Holy Land

from the Muslims. The First Crusade lasted from 1095 to 1099.

How many years separated parts one and two of Cervantes's *Don Quixote*?

Ten. Part One was published in 1605; Part Two in 1615.

What was Molière's real name?

Jean Baptiste Poquelin. Among the French playwright's works are *Tartuffe* (1664) and *The Misanthrope* (1666).

Who is *Le Bourgeois Gentilhomme*?

His name is Monsieur Jourdain, a well-to-do tradesman in the play written by Molière in 1670.

Why does Bluebeard kill his wives?

The title character of Charles Perrault's story "Barbe-bleue" (1697) kills his wives for looking into the locked room where he stores the corpses of other disobedient wives. His final wife, however, escapes Bluebeard's punishment.

Who is the unhappy Werther's beloved in Goethe's novel *The Sorrows of Young Werther* (1774; revised 1787)?

Lotte.

How many Wilhelm Meister novels did Goethe write?

The young man is the protagonist of two novels,

Wilhelm Meister's Apprenticeship (1795–96) and *Wilhelm Meister's Travels, or The Renunciants* (1829).

Where does the term *übermensch* first appear?

The German word for "overman" or "superperson" first appears in Goethe's *Faust* (1808,1833), referring to an extraordinarily gifted person. Nietzsche used the term for his transcendent man in *Thus Spake Zarathustra* (1883–91). The Nazis adopted the term as part of their doctrine of Aryan supremacy.

In *The Red and the Black*, what do the colors stand for?

In Stendhal's 1830 novel, the red refers to Napoleon's colors or the military life, the black to the clergy or religious life.

What happened to the concluding part of Nikolai Gogol's *Dead Souls* (1842)?

The first part is recognized as a comic masterpiece, but the second part never saw the light of day. Convinced by the radical priest Father Matthew Konstantinovsky that literature was sinful, Gogol (1809–52) burned the manuscript of Part Two in 1852. He died a few days later.

What Balzac novel did Fyodor Dostoyevsky translate into Russian?

Eugénie Grandet (1833). Dostoyevsky's 1844 translation was his first publication.

With whom did Guy de Maupassant (1850–93) study?
For nearly ten years the short story writer apprenticed himself to Flaubert to learn to write fiction.

What is a *rubaiyat*?
Rubaiyat is the plural of the Persian word meaning "a poem of four lines." *The Rubaiyat of Omar Khayyam of Naishapur* is a poem composed of such quatrains. The twelfth-century Persian poem was translated freely into English by Edward FitzGerald in 1859.

To whose funeral in 1885 did Tennyson send a wreath inscribed "To the World's Greatest Poet"?
The poet laureate of England sent the wreath to Victor Hugo's funeral. The author of the novel *Les Misérables* (1862) was also a great lyric poet. His poetic works included *Contemplations* (1856).

Where does the term "nihilist" first appear?
Russian writer Ivan Turgenev coined the word in his 1862 novel *Fathers and Sons*.

Whom does Raskolnikov murder in Dostoyevsky's *Crime and Punishment* (1866)?
The old pawnbroker Alena Ivanovna and her sister, Lizaveta.

In what war did Leo Tolstoy (1828–1910) serve?
He served in the Crimean War (1853–56), though he is best known for his treatment of the Napoleonic Wars in *War and Peace* (1863–69).

What are the seven sections of Marcel Proust's *À la recherche du temps perdu* (1913–27)?
Known in English as *Remembrance of Things Past*, the novel is divided as follows:
1. *Du côté de chez Swann* (*Swann's Way*)
2. *À l'ombre des jeunes filles en fleurs* (*Within a Budding Grove*)
3. *Le Côté de Guermantes* (*The Guermantes Way*)
4. *Sodome et Gomorrhe* (*Cities of the Plain*)
5. *La Prisonnière* (*The Captive*)
6. *Albertine disparue* or *La Fugitive* (*The Sweet Cheat Gone*)
7. *Le Temps retrouvé* (*The Past Recaptured*)

Where was author Marguerite Duras born?
Indochina, in 1914. The French writer is the author of the novel *The Lover* (1984) and the screenplay *Hiroshima, Mon Amour* (1960).

Which work of Franz Kafka's prefigures his story "The Metamorphosis" (1916)?
The story "Wedding Preparations in the Country" (1907) seems to directly foreshadow Gregor Samsa's plight, as a train passenger lying in bed imagines himself as a giant bug.

How old is Joseph K. in Kafka's *The Trial* (1925)?
The bank employee is arrested for no apparent reason on his thirtieth birthday.

Why does the Hunger Artist fast?
The alienated artist never discovered food that he en-

joyed, so he starves to death in Franz Kafka's short story "The Hunger Artist."

What was Colette's real name?
The French author of the novel *Chéri* (1920) was named Sidonie Gabrielle Claudine Colette.

What was the name of Chéri's lover in Colette's *Chéri* (1920)?
The young man Chéri is having an affair with is the aging courtesan Léonie Vallon, more commonly known as Léa de Lonval, or just Léa.

What was the nationality of Hermann Hesse?
The German-born author of *Siddhartha* (1922) and *Steppenwolf* (1927) became a Swiss citizen at the outbreak of World War I. He received the Nobel Prize in Literature in 1946.

How many novels did Vladimir Nabokov write in Russian before turning to English?
Ten, including *Laughter in the Dark* (1938). His first novel written in English was *The Real Life of Sebastian Knight* (1941). Nabokov (1899–1977) came to the United States in 1940 and was naturalized in 1945.

Where does Odysseus die in Nikos Kazantzakis's *The Odyssey: A Modern Sequel* (1938)?
The South Pole.

What family's and what village's history are recounted in Gabriel García Márquez's *One Hundred Years of Solitude* (1970)?
The novel tells the story of seven generations of the Buendía family in the village of Macondo.

In what language does Carlos Fuentes write?
Mexico's best-known author (*The Death of Artemio Cruz*, 1962; *The Old Gringo*, 1985) first began writing in English, but has since switched to his native language, Spanish.

Did Chilean poet Pablo Neruda live to see the 1973 coup by right-wing General Pinochet?
Just barely. Neruda died of a heart attack in Chile just twelve days after the coup. Neruda had supported the overthrown President Allende.

CRITICISM

According to Aristotle, what elements are necessary to a play?
There are six: plot, thought, character, diction, music, and spectacle.

According to Aristotle, what leads a writer to create?
Intuition and harmony. In the *Poetics* (335–322 B.C.), he writes: "[T]he instinct of intuition is implanted in man from childhood . . . and through intuition he learns his earliest lessons. . . . Next there is the instinct for 'harmony' and rhythm, meters being manifestly sections of rhythm."

When was Longinus's critical treatise *On the Sublime* published in Europe?
Not until 1554. The first-century essay was then translated into several languages and gained wide prominence, eventually influencing the poets of the eighteenth and nineteenth centuries.

Who coined the term "willing suspension of disbelief"?
Samuel Taylor Coleridge in his critical treatise *Biographia Literaria* (1817). Coleridge used the term to refer to the "poetic faith" of a reader in accepting imaginary elements in a literary work.

In what work did poet John Keats first employ the term "negative capability"?
In a letter written in December 1817 to his brothers George and Thomas, Keats first referred to *"negative capability*, that is when man is capable of being in uncertainties, Mysteries, doubts, without irritable reaching after fact and reason." Keats considered this quality essential to a "Man of Achievement especially in literature."

What is gusto and who defined the term?
In art, gusto is the excitement of the imagination that gives full expression to the dynamic character of an object. According to William Hazlitt (1778–1830) in his essay "On Gusto," gusto is "power or passion defining any object." Gusto unites the senses as "the impression made on one sense excites by affinity

those of another." Michelangelo's sculptures, says Hazlitt, "are full of gusto."

From what work did Matthew Arnold get the phrase "sweetness and light"?
From Jonathan Swift's *The Battle of the Books* (1704). Arnold used the phrase in *Culture and Anarchy* (1869) to elaborate his idea of culture as a humanizing and ennobling force.

How many rules of "literary art" did Mark Twain say James Fenimore Cooper violated in *The Deerslayer* (1841)?
In an 1895 article in *North American Review*, Twain said that Cooper violated 18 of the 19 rules for romantic fiction. On one page alone, Cooper is said to have scored a record-breaking 114 offenses out of a possible 115. Some of the rules Cooper broke included:
—"That a tale shall accomplish something and arrive somewhere."
—"[T]hat the episodes of a tale shall be necessary parts of the tale, and shall help to develop it."
—"[T]hat the personages in a tale shall be alive, except in the case of corpses, and that always the reader shall be able to tell the corpses from the others."

According to Leo Tolstoy (1828–1910), what is art?
In the 1898 essay "What is Art?" Tolstoy defines art as "a human activity, consisting in this, that one man consciously, by means of external signs, hands on to others feelings he has lived through, and that other

people are infected by these feelings, and also experience them."

Who led the critical movement of the "New Humanists"?

The leader of the intellectual group which, during the flowering of modernism, tried to spur interest in the classics, was Irving Babbitt, professor of romance languages at Harvard from 1894 to 1933.

Who originated the term "New Criticism"?

Literary critic Joel Spingarn in 1910 in an address at Columbia University called "The New Criticism." The term did not come into general use until John Crowe Ransom's book *The New Criticism* (1941). New Critics focused on the literary text as a discrete whole rather than on historical or biographical background.

How were critics Carl and Mark Van Doren related?

They were brothers. Both were members of the faculty of Columbia University, Carl from 1911 to 1930, Mark from 1920 to 1959.

What does I.A. stand for in I.A. Richards (1893–1979)?

The first and middle names of the twentieth-century English critic are Ivor Armstrong.

What critic coined the phrase the "American Renaissance"?

Francis Otto Matthiessen (1902–50), in his work *The American Renaissance: Art and Expression in the Age of*

Emerson and Whitman (1941). The phrase refers to a time in the mid-nineteenth century that saw a flourishing of talent in American letters.

What author was the subject of Northrop Frye's first book?

Frye's first book was *Fearful Symmetry: A Study of William Blake* (1947). The influential scholar is best known for his *Anatomy of Criticism* (1957), in which he introduced a critical system based on analysis of literary archetypes.

What is narratology?

Popularized in the 1960s by Roland Barthes and others, narratology is the study of narrative, linguistic or otherwise: myths, legends, novels, comic strips, stained-glass windows, psychological case studies. It employs methods drawn from structuralism, the study of the relations and functions of the internal elements of cultural phenomena.

What is the origin of the term "semiotics"?

Taken from the Greek word *semeion*, or "sign," the term had its origins early in the twentieth century, when French linguist Ferdinand de Saussure and American philosopher C. S. Peirce called for a new science of signs. Saussure called the discipline "semiology"; Peirce called it "semiotic." Since then, semiotics as the study of cultural sign systems (linguistic, visual, etc.) has come to replace the field once called structuralism.

What is "logocentrism"?
It is the habit of assigning truth to words. Deconstructionists seek to combat logocentrism by deconstructing, or taking apart, texts: exposing hidden presuppositions; revealing texts as essentially indeterminate and unreadable.

Where does Jacques Derrida teach?
Born in 1930, the French philosopher, critic, and founder of deconstructionism teaches at the École Normale Supérieure in Paris.

What is the correct pronunciation of the name Edward Said?
The surname of the Columbia professor who wrote *Orientalism* (1978) and *The World, the Text, and the Critic* (1983) is pronounced SAH-eed.

DEATHS

In what battle did Sir Philip Sidney suffer a mortal wound?
The Battle of Zutphen in 1586. The author of *Arcadia* (1590) was fighting in the Netherlands against the Spanish. He was shot in the thigh after lending his leg armor to another soldier. He died of infection three weeks later, at the age of thirty-two.

How did Thomas Chatterton (1752–70) die?
Chatterton was the author of several pseudo-fifteenth-century poems supposedly written by monk Thomas Rowley. He committed suicide in his London

garret by taking arsenic at age seventeen, driven to despair by poverty. He became a hero of native English verse to Romantic poets such as Wordsworth, Shelley, and Keats.

How did Edgar Allan Poe die?

In October 1849, the forty-year-old writer was found lying unconscious near a polling place in Baltimore. According to some reports, he had been fed liquor and dragged to various polling places to vote repeatedly. He was taken to a hospital where he remained semicomatose for three days. On October 7, at 3 A.M. he died of "congestion of the brain" and possibly intestinal inflammation, a weak heart, and diabetes.

What is Poe's epitaph?

"Quoth the Raven nevermore," from his poem "The Raven" (1845).

Where are Emerson, Thoreau, and Hawthorne buried?

In Sleepy Hollow Cemetery, Massachusetts.

How did poet Vachel Lindsay kill himself?

By drinking Lysol, in 1931 at age fifty-two.

How did Sherwood Anderson die?

The author of *Winesburg, Ohio* (1919) died of peritonitis after swallowing a toothpick at a cocktail party in 1941.

What epitaph did William Butler Yeats write for himself?
"Cast a cold eye
On life, on death.
Horseman, pass by!"
The epitaph appears on Yeats's tombstone in Drumcliff churchyard under a mountain called Ben Bulben in County Sligo, Ireland—just as Yeats wrote in his poem "Under Ben Bulben" (1939).

Where did Virginia Woolf drown herself?
The River Ouse near her home at Rodmell, Sussex, in 1941, following a bout with mental illness.

How did Margaret Mitchell die?
The author of *Gone With the Wind* (1936) died in 1949 at age forty-eight after being hit by a taxi in Atlanta.

When did John Berryman commit suicide?
On January 7, 1972. He jumped off a bridge into the Mississippi River. He was fifty-eight.

How did poet Dylan Thomas die?
He died at age thirty-nine in 1953 in New York City after drinking eighteen straight whiskeys in a bar and lapsing into a coma.

How did Jack Kerouac die?
The author of *On the Road* (1957) died at age forty-seven on October 21, 1969, of a massive gastric hemorrhage associated with alcoholism, in St. Petersburg, Florida.

How did William Burroughs kill his wife?
The author of *Naked Lunch* (1959) unsuccessfully attempted to shoot a glass off his wife's head.

How long after John Kennedy Toole's death was *A Confederacy of Dunces* published?
Eleven years. Born in 1937, Toole finished his comic novel of New Orleans in 1963, but failed to find a publisher. He committed suicide in 1969. With the help of the novelist Walker Percy, his mother succeeded in getting the book published in 1980. *Dunces* became a bestseller and won the 1981 Pulitzer Prize.

What were Hart Crane's last words?
"Goodbye, everybody!" He said it just before committing suicide by jumping off a ship in 1932.

DRAMA

What kind of shoes did Greek tragic actors wear?
They wore "buskins," boots that reached halfway up the calf and had thick soles to make the actors seem taller. The Greek word for the boot was *cothurnus.* "Buskin" first appeared as the English term in the sixteenth century.

Who was Clytemnestra's lover in Aeschylus's *Agamemnon* (458 B.C.)?
Aegisthus. He conspired with Clytemnestra to kill her husband, Agamemnon.

In what order did Sophocles write his three Theban tragedies?
Antigone was produced on stage first (441 B.C.), followed by *Oedipus the King* (c. 426 B.C.) and *Oedipus at Colonus* (first produced after the author's death in 405 B.C.). However, the story recounted by the plays follows a different order: *Oedipus the King* first; *Oedipus at Colonus* second; *Antigone* last.

Where is Colonus and what was Oedipus doing there?
In Sophocles' tragedy *Oedipus at Colonus* (c. 406 B.C.), the blinded Oedipus wanders by accident into the sacred grove of the furies at Colonus in Attica, about a mile northwest of Athens.

Which tragedy of Euripides was produced first: *Iphigenia in Aulis* or *Iphigenia in Tauris*?
Tauris came first, about 414–412 B.C.; *Aulis* followed about 405 B.C. In terms of the storyline, however, the order is reversed. *Aulis* tells of Agamemnon's decision to sacrifice his daughter Iphigenia in order to free the Greek fleet from the harbor at Aulis. *Tauris* tells of Iphigenia after the goddess Artemis snatches her to safety, and she is reunited with her brother Orestes in Tauris.

What are the major cycles of English mystery plays?
Four main collections of these plays based on biblical episodes survive:

> The York Cycle (early fourteenth century), forty-eight plays

The Towneley Cycle (mid-fourteenth–early fifteenth century), thirty-two plays
The Chester Cycle (fourteenth century), twenty-
four plays
The Coventry (or N Town) Cycle (fifteenth century), forty-three plays

Who goes with Everyman to face Judgment?
Only Good Deeds. In the 1495 morality play, Every-
man is deserted by Beauty, Strength, Discretion, and
Five Wits.

**Who first played Doctor Faustus in Christopher Mar-
lowe's tragedy?**
Edward Alleyn played the role in the original production, circa 1589. Alleyn also played the lead in Marlowe's *Tamburlaine the Great* (1587).

**What is the name of the title character in *The Alche-
mist*?**
Subtle is the name of the shady character in the 1610
play by Ben Jonson. He works with two other un-
savory characters, Face (a.k.a. Jeremy) and Dol
Common.

**How long has the Oberammergau Passion Play been
staged?**
It is said to have originated in 1633, when the people
of this village in Upper Bavaria vowed to stage it in
order to be rescued from the plague. The play depict-
ing Christ's passion is performed every tenth year.

When and where was Milton's masque *Comus* first performed?
It was first performed on Michaelmas Night (September 29), 1634, at Ludlow Castle to celebrate the Earl of Bridgewater's becoming Lord President of Wales and the Marches. The Earl's children enacted the roles of the Lady and her two brothers in the play.

What is closet drama?
It is a play, usually in verse, written for private reading rather than performance. Byron's *Manfred* (1817) and Shelley's *Prometheus Unbound* (1820) are examples.

When did the Abbey Theatre open?
The Dublin theater dedicated to presenting Irish drama opened in 1904. Its directors included William Butler Yeats and Lady Gregory. Destroyed by fire in 1951, the theater reopened in 1966.

In what year did J. M. Synge's *The Playboy of the Western World* spark a riot?
Rioting started during the first performance of the comedy at the Abbey Theatre in Dublin in 1907. The commotion was started by a reference to an undergarment.

Was there an actual Professor Henry Higgins, main character in George Bernard Shaw's *Pygmalion* (1913)?
The character was based on a British scholar of pho-

netics and Old English named Henry Sweet. His works included *History of English Sounds* (1874).

How does *Pygmalion* end?

The play ends with Eliza Doolittle asserting her humanity and rejecting Henry Higgins. But the 1938 movie ending, approved by Shaw, brought the pair together. The musical version, *My Fair Lady* (1956), also had a happy ending.

How many deceased inhabitants of Spoon River recite their verse epitaphs in Edgar Lee Masters's *Spoon River Anthology* (1915)?

Two hundred and forty-four.

On what novel is George Gershwin's opera *Porgy and Bess* (1935) based?

It is based on *Porgy* (1925), by Du Bose Heyward. Heyward and his wife, Dorothy, won a Pulitzer prize for their dramatic version of the novel. Porgy is a crippled beggar and gambler who lives on Catfish Row in Charleston, South Carolina. Bess is his drug-addicted mistress.

To what does the title of Sean O'Casey's *The Plough and the Stars* (1926) refer?

The banner of the Irish Citizens Army, of which O'Casey was once a member. The play concerns members of the army before and during the Easter Rising in 1916.

How did Jean Cocteau come up with the name of the character Heurtebise in the play *Orphée* (1926)?
The glazier Heurtebise (literally "break wind") aids the poet Orphée in rescuing his wife from Death. Cocteau has written that the name of Heurtebise was revealed to him in an opium-induced vision. The name obsessed Cocteau to the point that he thought another being was living inside him.

What is the setting of *The Front Page*?
The 1928 play about newspapers by Ben Hecht and Charles MacArthur is set in Chicago's Criminal Courts Building.

What was the source of Bertolt Brecht's *The Three-penny Opera* (1928)?
Brecht follows the general outline of English playwright John Gay's *The Beggar's Opera* (1728), but focuses more on social evils.

Who represents Agamemnon in Eugene O'Neill's *Mourning Becomes Electra* (1931)?
Ezra Mannon, a New England general returning from the Civil War. His wife Christine represents Clytemnestra.

What figure of Greek mythology is crushed by fate in Jean Cocteau's tragedy *The Infernal Machine* (1934)?
Oedipus.

What playwright wrote a play called *Paradise Lost* that was not based on Milton's poem?
Clifford Odets, in 1935. The play was about the fall of a middle-class family.

Who wrote *Arsenic and Old Lace*?
The 1941 Broadway play was written by Joseph Kesselring. The 1946 movie adaptation was directed by Frank Capra.

What is the last line of Jean-Paul Sartre's play *No Exit* (1944)?
"Well, let's get on with it. . . ." It is spoken by Garcia when he realizes he is facing eternity.

On what work did Tennessee Williams base *The Glass Menagerie* (1944)?
The Broadway play was drawn from a screenplay called *The Gentleman Caller*, which Williams wrote while he was under contract as a screenwriter for MGM in the early 1940s.

How long was the first run of Tennessee Williams's *A Streetcar Named Desire* (1947)?
The play opened in New York in 1947 and ran for 855 performances.

Who first played Blanche DuBois in the first production?
Jessica Tandy, opposite Marlon Brando as Stanley Kowalski.

What work by Christopher Isherwood was the basis for the musical _Cabaret_ (1968)?
Cabaret was based on the play _I Am a Camera_ (1951) by John Van Druten, which was in turn based on Isherwood's "Sally Bowles," a story appearing in _Goodbye to Berlin_ (1939). Isherwood lived in Berlin in the early 1930s.

What is the setting of Samuel Beckett's _Waiting for Godot_ (1953)?
The only scenery is a tree, leafless in Act 1, and with leaves in Act 2.

What is unusual about Samuel Beckett's 1970 play _Breath_?
The thirty-second piece has no actors and no dialogue.

What play did Maya Angelou write and produce with actor Godfrey Cambridge?
The two collaborated on _Cabaret for Freedom_ in 1960. Cambridge is best known for his appearances in films like _Watermelon Man_ (1970) and _Cotton Comes to Harlem_ (1970). Angelou's poetry, prose, and drama include the autobiographical volume, _I Know Why the Caged Bird Sings_ (1969).

What is the opening line of Edward Albee's play _Who's Afraid of Virginia Woolf_ (1962)?
"Jesus H. Christ" is the first line of the play, and the first of many profanities in Albee's look into a de-

structive marriage. A London production changed the first line to "Mary H. Magdalen."

What is Neil Simon's complete name and what was his first Broadway play?
Marvin Neil Simon's (1927–   ) first Broadway play was *Barefoot in the Park*, about a young married couple living in New York City. It was produced in 1963.

Where was *The Sign in Sidney Brustein's Window*?
In the 1964 play of the same name by Lorraine Hansberry, it was located in Greenwich Village, New York City.

What was Sam Shepard's first play?
It was *The Tooth of Crime* (1973). His later plays include *Buried Child* (1979) and *True West* (1980).

What is the longest-running play in theater history?
It is *The Mousetrap* (1952) by Agatha Christie, which has never closed on the British stage. It was adapted from one of Christie's stories.

How long has *The Fantasticks* been running?
The musical by Tom Jones and Harvey Schmidt has been running for over thirty years, since May 1960.

ENGLISH
LITERATURE

When was English first spoken in England?
Not until 449, when three Germanic tribes from Denmark—the Jutes, Angles, and Saxons—invaded Britain. The Angles, who settled along the east coast of north and central England, developed literate culture and gave their name to the country (Angle-land, England). The language of these tribes, Anglo-Saxon or Old English, is the precursor of modern English.

In the Old English poem *Beowulf* (eighth cent.), what nation did Beowulf come from?
The Geats, a Scandinavian people.

What was a summoner? A canon's yeoman? A franklin? A manciple? A reeve?
These occupations of characters in Chaucer's *Canterbury Tales* (c. 1387–1400) refer to the following:
   summoner—an officer who summoned suspects before the ecclesiastical courts
   canon's yeoman—an attendant of a canon; a canon was a clergyman associated with a cathedral or large church
   franklin—a prosperous country man of low birth
   manciple—a steward of a community of lawyers
   reeve—a superintendent of a large farming estate

When was Chaucer's *Troilus and Criseyde* written?
Between 1385–90.

When was Shakespeare's *Troilus and Cressida* written?
It was first performed around 1602 and first published in 1609.

When did Holinshed write his chronicles?
Raphael Holinshed's *Chronicles of England, Scotland, and Ireland* appeared in 1577. This history was Shakespeare's source for much of *Macbeth, King Lear,* and *Cymbeline.* Holinshed died about 1580.

What virtues and what knights are the subjects of each of the six books of Spenser's *The Faerie Queene* (1596)?
   Book I: Holiness/The Red Cross Knight
   Book II: Temperance/Guyon
   Book III: Chastity/Britomart

Book IV: Friendship/Cambel and Triamond
Book V: Justice/Artegall
Book VI: Courtesy/Calidore

What does the title *Novum Organum* mean?
The title of Francis Bacon's 1620 philosophical treatise means literally "new instrument." It alludes to Aristotle's treatise on logic and the theory of science, commonly known as the *Organon*.

What is Milton's companion work to "L'Allegro"?
"Il Penseroso," written in 1632.

Who was commemorated in Milton's elegy *Lycidas* (1637)?
Edward King, a college friend from Cambridge who had become a clergyman. He drowned in 1637.

How many years separated the publication of Milton's *Paradise Lost* and its sequel, *Paradise Regained*?
Four. The first was published in 1667, the latter in 1671.

What is the time span of *Samson Agonistes* (1671)?
The tragedy by John Milton, about Samson's battle of faith and destruction of the Philistine temple, spans one day.

In John Dryden's poem "Absalom and Achitophel" (1681), what contemporary political figures do the title characters represent?
In the Bible, Absalom is the son of King David

spurred to rebellion by Achitophel. In Dryden's satire, Absalom represents the Duke of Monmouth, the illegitimate son of King Charles II, while Achitophel is the Earl of Shaftesbury.

Whom did John Dryden refer to as "Mac Flecknoe" in his 1682 poem of the same name?

Thomas Shadwell, a playwright whose work Dryden despised. Dryden satirized Shadwell as the son of ("Mac") Richard Flecknoe, another bad contemporary poet.

When were the first and second Augustan Ages?

The first was in the time of the Roman emperor Augustus (27 B.C.–14 A.D.), when Latin poets like Vergil, Ovid, and Horace brought about a literary golden age. The second was in the early to mid-eighteenth century in England, when writers such as Alexander Pope, Jonathan Swift, and Richard Steele ushered in their own period of high literary style under Queen Anne, drawing on Roman models.

How do you spell the name Swift gave to his race of rational horses in *Gulliver's Travels* (1726)?

Houyhnhnms. Their subjects, a race of nasty human-like creatures, had an easier name: Yahoos.

At whom was Alexander Pope's poem *The Dunciad* (1728) aimed?

Published in several versions from 1728 to 1743, the mock-epic poem satirized bad writing and attacked critics of Pope's poetry. In the final version, the king of the Dunces is Colley Cibber, England's Poet Laureate from 1730 to 1757. Other targets of Pope's venom were dramatists Nahum Tate and Lewis Theobald.

Whom did novelist Henry Fielding summon to court for the murder of the English language?
Poet laureate Colley Cibber in 1740. Fielding issued the summons under the pseudonym "Captain Hercules Vinegar."

What was Pamela's last name in Samuel Richardson's *Pamela* (1740)?
Andrews.

What was Shamela's last name in Henry Fielding's parody *Shamela* (1741)?
It was also Andrews. The name was used a third time in Fielding's *Joseph Andrews* (1742), the story of Pamela's brother, Joseph.

Who was Tom Jones's mother?
At the beginning of Fielding's novel *Tom Jones* (1749), it appears his mother is Jenny Jones, servant of Squire Allworthy. By the end of the novel, his true mother is revealed: Bridget, Squire Allworthy's sister.

Who narrates Laurence Sterne's *A Sentimental Journey Through France and Italy* (1768)?
Mr. Yorick, a character from Sterne's earlier novel *Tristram Shandy* (1767).

Who wrote "Auld Lang Syne"?
Scottish poet Robert Burns (1759–96) put this traditional song into its present form in *The Scots Musical Museum* (1787–1803).

Who or what was "Udolpho" in Ann Radcliffe's Gothic novel *The Mysteries of Udolpho* (1794)?
It was the castle of the evil Montoni in the Italian Apennines, and site of many scary events.

What is the first poem of *Lyrical Ballads* (1798) by Wordsworth and Coleridge?
The first poem in what many consider the founding work of English romanticism is Coleridge's "The Rime of the Ancient Mariner."

What is the last?
The last is Wordsworth's "Lines Composed a Few Miles Above Tintern Abbey."

What are Sir Walter Scott's "Waverley Novels"?
These romances about life in Scotland were published anonymously by Scott under the credit "the author of Waverley." The first book, *Waverley*, appeared in 1814 and helped to shift Scott's career from poetry to fiction. The Waverley novels include:
Guy Mannering (1815)
Old Mortality (1816)
Rob Roy (1818)
The Heart of Midlothian (1818)
The Bride of Lammermoor (1819)

What was the alternative title to Mary Shelley's *Frankenstein* (1818)?
The Modern Prometheus.

What does *Sartor Resartus* mean?
The title of Carlyle's 1833–34 satire on German philosophy means "the tailor retailored" in Latin. It comments on the work of the fictitious Diogenes Teufelsdröckh, philosopher of clothes.

What Charles Dickens novel exposed the "ragged schools" and helped get them abolished?
Nicholas Nickleby (1838–39).

In what business were Dombey and Son?
In Dickens's 1847–48 novel of that name, Dombey and Son was a shipping firm.

How many historical novels did Charles Dickens write?
Two: *A Tale of Two Cities* (1859), set in London and Paris during the French Revolution, and *Barnaby Rudge* (1841), set during the anti-Catholic riots sparked by Lord George Gordon in 1780.

What was the interminable law case in Dickens's *Bleak House* (1852–53)?
Jarndyce v. Jarndyce, a case stemming from a dispute about distribution of an estate.

Who wrote *The Life of Charlotte Brontë* (1857)?
Her close friend, novelist Elizabeth Gaskell. The two met in 1850; Brontë died five years later.

What is the name of Rochester's house in Charlotte Brontë's *Jane Eyre* (1847)?
Thornfield Hall.

What is the name of Miss Havisham's house in Dickens's *Great Expectations* (1860-61)?
Satis House.

What is the Mill on the Floss?
It is the Dorlcote Mill, located in St. Ogg's on the River Floss. It is owned by Edward Tulliver, father of Maggie Tulliver, central character of George Eliot's 1860 novel, *The Mill on the Floss*.

What is Daisy Miller's real name?
Annie Miller. She appears in Henry James's short novel *Daisy Miller* (1878).

What are the names of the ghosts in Henry James's *The Turn of the Screw* (1898)?
Peter Quint and Miss Jessel, the former valet and governess at the estate called Bly.

What is Tess's name before she becomes Tess of the d'Urbervilles?
She is Tess Durbeyfield, daughter of Jack Durbeyfield, a carter. In the 1891 novel by Thomas Hardy, *Tess of the d'Urbervilles*, she eventually becomes the kept woman of Alec d'Urbervilles, a member of the well-to-do family for whom she is working.

How many years before his death did Thomas Hardy publish his last novel?
Thirty-three. Hardy's last novel was *Jude the Obscure*

(1895), the story of Jude Fawley's adulterous love for his cousin Sue Bridehead. The novel so shocked readers that Hardy gave up writing fiction and turned to poetry. Hardy died in 1928.

In H. G. Wells's novel, what is the name of the Invisible Man?
Griffin. *The Invisible Man* was published in 1897. Griffin remains invisible until he is dying.

What was Saki's real name?
H. H. Munro (1870–1916). The Scottish fiction writer and playwright was born in Burma and killed by a sniper in France during World War I.

When did Conrad make the journey down the Congo River that became the basis for *Heart of Darkness* (1902)?
In 1890, aboard the *Roi des Belges*. Conrad took over as ship master when the captain fell ill of tropical fever.

What is the subtitle of Conrad's *Nostromo* (1904)?
A Tale of the Seaboard.

> **What is the epigraph for Conrad's *Nostromo*?**
> "So foul a sky clears not without a storm" (Shakespeare).

What was Virginia Woolf's maiden name?
Adeline Virginia Stephen. She married Leonard Woolf in 1912.

What gave the Bloomsbury Group its name?
The group of writers and thinkers, which included Virginia Woolf, Vanessa Bell, and Lytton Strachey, among others, was named for the place where they held their meetings—46 Gordon Square, in Bloomsbury, London.

When is Bloomsday?
Bloomsday—the date on which James Joyce's *Ulysses* (1922) is set—is June 16, 1904.

What book about the Holy Grail quest did T. S. Eliot draw upon in his poem, *The Waste Land* (1922)?
Jessie L. Weston's *From Ritual to Romance* (1920).

What was the original title of James Joyce's *Finnegans Wake*?
It was called *Work in Progress* during the seventeen years of its composition (1922–39). Parts of it were published under that title before the work was completed.

What was George Orwell's real name?
Eric Arthur Blair.

Who were the Angry Young Men?
A group of British playwrights and novelists in the 1950s, including John Osborne, Kingsley Amis, and Alan Sillitoe. Their politics were left-wing; their favorite theme was alienation.

What is the name of the language spoken by the teenage gangs in *A Clockwork Orange* (1962)?
The mixture of Russian with American and British slang is called "Nadsat."

For what magazine did Julian Barnes write a gossip column?
In the 1970s, the author of *Flaubert's Parrot* (1984) wrote the "Edward Pygge" gossip column for the British periodical, *The New Review*.

What relation are Kingsley Amis and Martin Amis?
They are father and son. Kingsley Amis's books include *Lucky Jim* (1954) and *Jake's Thing* (1978); Martin Amis's novels include *Success* (1978) and *Money* (1984).

FAMOUS
PHRASES

Who asked, "Was this the face that launched a thousand ships, /And burnt the topless towers of Ilium"?
Dr. Faustus in Christopher Marlowe's play *Dr. Faustus* (c. 1588–92), on conjuring up Helen of Troy.

Who said, "My mind to me a kingdom is"?
Sir Edward Dyer in his 1588 poem of the same name.

Who wrote, "Go and catch a falling star,/Get with child a mandrake root"?
John Donne (1572?–1631), in the opening lines to the

poem, "Song," which was published posthumously, in 1633.

Who said, "Gather ye rosebuds while ye may"?
Robert Herrick, in the first line of the 1648 poem "To the Virgins, to Make Much of Time."

> **Whom did Herrick urge to go a-Maying?**
> Corinna, in "Corinna's Going A-Maying" (1648).

Who wrote, "To err is human, to forgive divine"?
Alexander Pope's expression of charity appears in *An Essay on Criticism* (1711).

> **In what Pope poem is reference made to "damning with faint praise"?**
> The "Epistle to Dr. Arbuthnot" (1735). In the satiric poem, Pope wrote: "Damn with faint praise, assent with civil leer,/And, without sneering, teach the rest to sneer."

What author said of what work, "I have protracted my work til most of those whom I wished to please have sunk into the grave, and success and miscarriage are empty sounds: I therefore dismiss it with frigid tranquility, having little to fear or hope from censure or from praise"?
Dr. Samuel Johnson said it of his dictionary in "Preface to *A Dictionary of the English Language*" (1747–55).

Who wrote "These are the times that try men's souls"?
Thomas Paine in "The American Crisis," a series of pamphlets he published between 1776 and 1783.

When he wrote the opening sentence to the first pamphlet, the Revolutionary army had just retreated across New Jersey and defeat seemed imminent.

Who first called the press the "fourth estate"?
Eighteenth-century political philosopher Edmund Burke is credited with the term. Burke is supposed to have said, "Yonder [in the Reporters' Gallery] sits the fourth estate, more important than them all." The three other estates were the Lords Spiritual (clergy), the Lords Temporal (knights and barons), and the Commons.

Who wrote "O, my luve's like a red, red rose/That's newly sprung in June"?
Robert Burns in "A Red, Red Rose" (1796).

Who wrote "O rose, thou art sick"?
William Blake in "The Sick Rose" (1794).

Who wrote "Water, Water, everywhere/Nor any drop to drink"?
Samuel Taylor Coleridge in his poem "The Rime of the Ancient Mariner" (1798). The lines are often misquoted as "and not a drop to drink."

What poem contains the line "Beauty is truth, truth beauty"?
Keats's "Ode on a Grecian Urn" (1819).

Who said "The Child is father of the Man"?
William Wordsworth, in the poem "My Heart Leaps Up When I Behold" (1807).

What poet wrote as his own epitaph, "Here lies one whose name was writ in water"?
John Keats, who died at the age of twenty-five, believing his art would not be remembered.

What Edward Bulwer-Lytton novel begins, "It was a dark and stormy night"?
Paul Clifford (1830). It is also the opening line of numerous novels by Snoopy.

What does "in a Pickwickian sense" mean?
It refers to the joking use of insulting words or epithets. The phrase comes from Dickens's *Pickwick Papers* (1836–37). Samuel Pickwick exchanges barbs in just such a friendly way with Mr. Blotton in Chapter One.

What is the source of the phrase "What hath God wrought"?
It comes from the Bible, Numbers 23:23. It is now best known as the first message sent by telegraph, May 28, 1844.

How many times does Poe's Raven say "Nevermore"?
The "ungainly fowl" quoths "Nevermore" six times in "The Raven," first published in 1845.

Who wrote "That government is best which governs least"?
Henry David Thoreau, in his essay, "Civil Disobedience" (1849).

What poem ends with: "And we are here as on a darkling plain/Swept with confused alarms of struggle and flight,/Where ignorant armies clash by night"?
Matthew Arnold's "Dover Beach" (c. 1851).

Who first used the expression "the Almighty Dollar"?
Washington Irving is believed to have originated it in *Wolfert's Roost* (1855).

Who wrote "A Jug of Wine, a Loaf of Bread—and Thou"?
Twelfth-century Persian poet Omar Khayyam in his *Rubaiyat*, translated into English by Edward Fitz-Gerald in 1859.

Who wrote "Shoot, if you must, this old gray head"?
John Greenleaf Whittier describes the bravery of the fictional title character in his poem "Barbara Frietchie" (1863). The aged Frietchie displays a Union flag when Confederate troops march by. Stonewall Jackson forbids his troops to harm the old woman.

Which work by Oscar Wilde includes the statement "I can resist everything except temptation"?
Lady Windermere's Fan (1892).

What poet in what poem says "I am the master of my fate/I am the captain of my soul"?
William Ernest Henley (1849–1903) in "Invictus."

What prompted Mark Twain to say "The reports of my death are greatly exaggerated"?
In 1897, Twain was in seclusion, grieving over a death in the family, when a sensationalistic newspaper reported that he had died impoverished in London. When a reporter appeared at Twain's home, the writer read a prepared statement containing the famous line.

What did Henry James call "the Distinguished Thing"?
Death. James used the phrase when he said "so it has come at last—the Distinguished Thing" after suffering a stroke on December 2, 1915, two months before his death in 1916.

What poet wrote "good fences make good neighbors"?
Robert Frost in the 1914 poem "Mending Wall":
"And he likes having thought of it so well/
He says again, 'Good fences make good neighbors.' "

Who wrote: "Laugh, and the world laughs with you,/ Weep, and you weep alone"?
They are the opening lines of the poem "Solitude" by Ella Wheeler Wilcox (1855–1919).

Where does the phrase "gone with the wind" come from?
The title of Margaret Mitchell's 1936 novel comes from a poem by Ernest Dowson, a poet of the 1890s, called "Non Sum Qualis Eram," or "Cynara."

Who coined the term "the lost generation"?
Gertrude Stein. She translated the phrase from a French garage proprietor who was angry at a young mechanic's negligence in fixing Stein's car. Stein used it to refer to Hemingway and his contemporaries: "All of you young people who served in the war. You are a lost generation." The term came to mean the rootless, disillusioned generation that came of age between World War I and the Great Depression.

What poem contains the line, "Things fall apart; the center cannot hold"?
William Butler Yeats's "The Second Coming" (1920).

Where did the English title for Marcel Proust's À la recherche du temps perdu (1913–27) come from?
C. K. Scott Moncrieff took the title *Remembrance of Things Past* for his 1922 English translation of Proust from Shakespeare's Sonnet 30: "When to the sessions of sweet silent thought/I summon up remembrance of things past." The literal translation of Proust's title is "In Search of Lost Time."

What is the quotation at the start of T. S. Eliot's poem "The Hollow Men" (1925)?
"Mistah Kurtz—he dead," from Joseph Conrad's novel *Heart of Darkness*.

Who wrote "Men seldom make passes/At girls who wear glasses"?
Dorothy Parker, known for her sharp wit, wrote the famous couplet in the poem "News Item" in 1926.

FAMOUS PHRASES

What poem is the source of the title of Robert Penn Warren's *World Enough and Time* (1950)?
Andrew Marvell's "To His Coy Mistress" (1681).

What is Rhett Butler's parting shot to Scarlett O'Hara in Margaret Mitchell's *Gone With the Wind* (1936)?
"My dear, I don't give a damn." In the 1939 movie, it became, "Frankly, my dear, I don't give a damn."

Who wrote, "Hell is—other people"?
Jean-Paul Sartre in his existential play *No Exit* (1944).

Who said, "A poem should not mean/But be"?
Archibald Macleish (1892–1982) in *Ars Poetica*.

What Langston Hughes poem refers to a "raisin in the sun"?
"Harlem" (1951). Hughes asks:
"What happens to a dream deferred?
Does it dry up
like a raisin in the sun?"

What poem says the world ends "Not with a bang but a whimper"?
T. S. Eliot's "The Hollow Men" (1925).

FICTION

Who called the novel a "comic-epic poem in prose"?
Henry Fielding (1707–54), in the preface to his 1742 novel *Joseph Andrews*.

Who created Roderick Random?
Tobias Smollett, in *The Adventures of Roderick Random* (1748).

Who created Roderick Usher?
Edgar Allan Poe, in "The Fall of the House of Usher" (1839).

Who created Roderick Hudson?
Henry James, in the 1876 novel of the same name.

What novel is subtitled "A Novel Without a Hero"?
Thackeray's *Vanity Fair* (1848).

What is the full title of Dickens's *David Copperfield* (1849–50)?
The Personal History, Experience and Observations of David Copperfield the Younger, of Blunderstone Rookery, Which He Never Meant To Be Published On Any Account.

Of *Oliver Twist* (1838)?
Oliver Twist, or, The Parish Boy's Progress.

Of *The Pickwick Papers* (1836–37)?
The Posthumous Papers of the Pickwick Club.

What was George Sand's real name?
The French author of *Consuelo* (1842) was born Amandine Lucie Aurore Dupin.

What was George Eliot's real name?
The English author of *Middlemarch* (1871–72) was born Mary Ann Evans.

What is the subtitle of Melville's short story "Bartleby the Scrivener" (1853)?
"A Story of Wall Street."

What was the last work of Herman Melville published in his lifetime?
The satire of America, called *The Confidence Man*, was published in 1857 to little public notice. Melville died in 1891.

Who wrote "The Lady or the Tiger?"
Frank Stockton wrote the story in 1882.

> **Which comes out of the door at the end—the lady or the tiger?**
> It is not revealed.

From what year was Edward Bellamy looking backward in *Looking Backward* (1888)?
The year 2000.

> **What is the sequel to Edward Bellamy's *Looking Backward*?**
> *Equality* (1897).

In what work did Joseph Conrad define his task as a writer as, "to make you hear, to make you feel—it is, before all, to make you *see*!"?
In the preface to *The Nigger of the Narcissus* (1897).

What books comprise John Galsworthy's *The Forsyte Saga*?
Three novels:
1. *The Man of Property* (1906)
2. *In Chancery* (1920)
3. *To Let* (1921)

and two "interludes":
1. *Indian Summer of a Forsyte* (1922)
2. *Awakenings* (1922)

Who are the three subjects of Gertrude Stein's *Three Lives* (1909)?
"The Good Anna" is about a German servant,

"Melanctha" is about a young black woman, and "The Gentle Lena" is about a German maid.

What is the last name of Ántonia in Willa Cather's novel *My Ántonia* (1918)?

Her full name is Ántonia Shimerda, eldest daughter of a Bohemian family in Black Hawk, Nebraska.

Who wrote the novel *The Magnificent Ambersons* (1918)?

Orson Welles's 1942 movie was based on the Pulitzer Prize–winning novel by Booth Tarkington. Tarkington also won a Pulitzer for the novel *Alice Adams* (1921).

What is Mrs. Dalloway's first name?

Clarissa. Virginia Woolf's novel *Mrs. Dalloway* was published in 1925.

In Don Marquis's "archy and mehitabel" stories, which is the cockroach and which the cat?

Archy is the cockroach, Mehitabel the cat. Archy was said to have written the stories at night on newspaper columnist Marquis's typewriter. He wrote without capitals because he couldn't reach the shift key. The stories were first collected in *archy and mehitabel* (1927).

What does Virginia Woolf mean by "a room of one's own"?

In the 1928 essay of the same name, it refers to the space a woman needs to write fiction. Specifically,

Woolf says that a woman needs two things to be able to write: "money and a room of her own." The essay was drawn from two papers Woolf gave at the Arts Society at Newnham and the Odtaa at Girton in 1928 on the subject of women and fiction.

Did Zelda Fitzgerald write any novels?
One, *Save Me the Waltz* (1932).

Which came first, *1984* or *Brave New World*?
Aldous Huxley's *Brave New World* was published in 1932, George Orwell's *1984* in 1949.

How many sequels to *I, Claudius* (1934) did Robert Graves write?
One, *Claudius the God*, published in 1934. It charts Claudius's rule from 41 A.D. until his poisoning by his wife Agrippina in 54 A.D.

What did Zora Neale Hurston do before becoming a novelist?
Hurston was a folklorist who studied with anthropologist Franz Boas at Barnard College. In *Mules and Men* (1935) and *Tell My Horse* (1938), she compiled black traditions of the South and the Caribbean. Her novels include *Their Eyes Were Watching God* (1937).

Who is Finnegan in *Finnegans Wake* (1939)?
He is an Irish hod carrier who dies after a fall. At his wake, he is momentarily returned to life at the mention of the word "whiskey." The name also refers to

legendary Irish hero Finn MacCool, who is supposed to "wake again" someday to save Ireland.

What fantasy opens James Thurber's short story "The Secret Life of Walter Mitty" (1942)?
Mild-mannered Walter Mitty imagines that he is a Navy hydroplane commander flying through a howling storm.

Where was novelist Jamaica Kincaid born?
St. John's, Antigua, in the West Indies, in 1949. Her given name is Elaine Potter Richardson.

What is the source of the title _The Catcher in the Rye_ (1951)?
It is a reference to Robert Burns's poem "Comin' Through the Rye" (1792), which Holden Caulfield quotes.

How does Bernard Malamud's _The Natural_ (1952) end?
Unlike the 1988 film adaptation, in which Roy Hobbs wins the World Series with a pyrotechnic home run, Malamud's original story has the slugger, preoccupied with sex and materialism, throw the final game of the World Series.

What is the name of the minor-league team in Mark Harris's _Bang the Drum Slowly_ (1956)?
The New York Mammoths. The novel's narrator is Henry Wiggen, star pitcher for the Mammoths.

What is meant by the title of William Burroughs's novel *Naked Lunch* (1959)?
The title to the drug-induced stream-of-consciousness narrative means a "frozen moment when everyone sees what is on the end of every fork" and is repulsed by it. The title was suggested to the author by Jack Kerouac.

What is the first movie mentioned by name in Walker Percy's *The Moviegoer* (1961)?
Stagecoach (1939), directed by John Ford.

What is the second?
The Third Man (1949), directed by Carol Reed.

How many members were there in Mary McCarthy's Group?
Her 1963 novel *The Group* concerns eight women students at Vassar. Their names are: Dottie, Helena, Kay, Lakey, Libby, Pokey, Polly, and Priss.

Who wrote *The Bell Jar*?
The novel of attempted suicide and recovery was written by Sylvia Plath, but was first published under the pseudonym of Victoria Lucas in 1963. It did not appear under the author's name until 1966.

What was Anne Tyler's first novel?
If Morning Ever Comes (1965), written in her early twenties. Born in 1941, Tyler was respected by critics but did not become widely known until *Dinner at the Homesick Restaurant* in 1982.

FICTION

What Kurt Vonnegut novel features science-fiction writer Kilgore Trout?
Trout is a recurring character in Vonnegut's books, including *God Bless You, Mr. Rosewater* (1965), *Slaughterhouse-Five* (1969), *Breakfast of Champions* (1973), and *Jailbird* (1979).

What is the subtitle of Kurt Vonnegut's *Slaughterhouse-Five*?
The Children's Crusade: A Duty-Dance with Death.

How many novels has James Dickey written?
Two—*Deliverance* (1970) and *Alnilam* (1987). Dickey also wrote the screenplay for the 1972 movie *Deliverance*, and appeared in the film as a sheriff. A poet and critic, Dickey received the National Book Award for poetry in 1966 for *Bucketdancer's Choice* (1965).

What is the first line of Philip Roth's *The Great American Novel* (1973)?
"Call me Smitty." Through his narrator, Word Smith, Roth not only spoofs Melville, but Hawthorne, Twain, Hemingway, and all other writers who pursued the Great American Novel.

With whom does Kugelmass have an affair in Woody Allen's short story "The Kugelmass Episode" (1977)?
Emma Bovary. The Great Persky projects the bored professor into Flaubert's *Madame Bovary* (1856) and Emma Bovary into modern Manhattan.

In what year is C. J. Koch's *The Year of Living Dangerously* (1978) set?
In 1965, the year of Suharto's overthrow of Sukarno's Indonesian government.

How many new Barbara Pym novels have been published since her death in 1980?
Four:
1. *A Few Green Leaves* (1980)
2. *An Unsuitable Attachment* (1982)
3. *Crampton Hodnet* (1985)
4. *An Academic Question* (1986)

A memoir, *A Very Private Eye*, was published in 1984.

Whose letters make up Alice Walker's novel *The Color Purple* (1982)?
The novel is comprised of letters from a black Southern woman named Celie to God, her sister, Nettie, and a missionary in Africa, and of Nettie's letters to Celie.

What is Toni Morrison's real name?
The author of the novels *Song of Solomon* (1977) and *Beloved* (1987) was born Chloe Anthony Wofford.

Who is killed at the beginning of E. L. Doctorow's novel *Billy Bathgate* (1989)?
Bo Weinberg, Dutch Schultz's former henchman. By Schultz's orders, he is thrown off a ship with his feet encased in cement.

FIRSTS
AND LASTS

What was the first book printed in English?
The Recuyell of the Historyes of Troye, a prose romance
by Raoul Lefevre, printed by William Caxton in 1474
in Bruges, Belgium. Caxton himself translated it from
the French. Caxton also printed the first dated book
printed in English, *Dictes and Sayenges of the Phyloso-
phers*, published on November 18, 1477.

**What was the first complete English translation of
the Bible?**
It was the Bible of 1380, translated into a Midland
dialect by Nicholas of Hereford and others. It is often

called the Wyclif Bible, though theologian John Wyclif (c. 1320–84) did not work on it.

Who was the first female professional author in English?
Aphra Behn (1640–89), author of the play *The Rover* (1677) and the novel *Oroonoko* (1688). She wrote under the pseudonym Astrea.

Who was the first poet laureate of England?
While James I granted a pension to Ben Jonson in 1616, it was not until 1668 that the laureateship was created as a royal office. John Dryden (1631–1700) was appointed by Charles II and held the office until 1688, when he was stripped of the laureateship by William and Mary because he had become a Catholic and had supported James II.

Who established the first literary club in America?
Author Anne Hutchinson organized literary groups for women in the seventeenth century.

When was the first copyright act passed?
The first national copyright act was passed in England in 1709.

Who first used the phrase "belles lettres" in English?
Jonathan Swift in *Tatler* 230 (1710): "The Traders in History and Politics, and the Belles Lettres." In French the term means "beautiful letters, fine writing." Swift added the pejorative connotation of light or trivial literature.

What was the first play produced in America?
The Recruiting Officer, by British playwright George
Farquhar, was produced on December 6, 1732, in
New York.

What was the first novel to sell a million copies?
Harriet Beecher Stowe's *Uncle Tom's Cabin* (1852).

What was the first work Dickens read publicly?
A Christmas Carol on June 30, 1857, at St. Martin's
Hall, London.

What are the first words of *War and Peace* (1864–69)?
"Well, Prince, so Genoa and Lucca are now just fam-
ily estates of the Buonapartes." Anna Pavlovna
Scherer says it to Prince Vasili Kuragin.

What were Henry David Thoreau's last words?
"Moose, Indian," spoken on his deathbed on May 6,
1862. Their meaning is not known.

What were Anton Chekhov's last words?
Chekhov, born in 1860, died of tuberculosis on July 2,
1904. While on his deathbed, he was prescribed a
glass of champagne to stimulate his heart. Taking the
glass, the playwright said his last words to his wife:
"It is some time since I drank champagne."

**Who was the first American to be honored with a
bust in Poets' Corner, Westminster Abbey?**
Henry Wadsworth Longfellow, following his death in
1882.

What is the final word of *Ulysses* (1922)?
The last seven words of Molly Bloom's extended interior monologue are "yes I said yes I will Yes."

What was William Faulkner's first published book?
The Marble Faun, a volume of poetry, was published in 1924.

What was Isak Dinesen's first book?
Seven Gothic Tales, published in 1934. *Out of Africa* was published in 1937.

What was the first major American company devoted solely to publishing paperbacks?
It was Pocket Books, founded in 1939. The first ten books the company published were:
1. *Wake Up and Live!*, Dorothea Brande
2. *Wuthering Heights*, Emily Brontë
3. *The Way of All Flesh*, Samuel Butler
4. *The Murder of Roger Ackroyd*, Agatha Christie
5. *Lost Horizon*, James Hilton
6. *Enough Rope*, Dorothy Parker
7. *Bambi*, Felix Salten
8. *Five Great Tragedies*, William Shakespeare
9. *Topper*, Thorne Smith
10. *The Bridge of San Luis Rey*, Thornton Wilder

What is the last sentence of *Finnegans Wake* (1939)?
The last, incomplete sentence is, "A way a lone a last a loved a long the"

What is the first?
The first is also incomplete, and may serve as the completion of the last: "riverrun, past Eve and Adam's, from swerve of shore to bend of bay, brings us by a commodius vicus of recirculation back to Howth Castle and Environs."

What was the first all-paperback bookstore?
It is City Lights Bookstore, opened in San Francisco in 1953 by poet Lawrence Ferlinghetti (1919–   ). It is still in operation, carrying both hard- and softcover books.

Who was the first U.S. poet laureate?
Robert Penn Warren was appointed to the newly created post in 1986. American poet laureates serve one-year terms rather than life terms as in England. Richard Wilbur, Howard Nemerov, Mark Strand, Joseph Brodsky, and Mona Van Duyn have held the post since then.

What was J. D. Salinger's last published work?
"Hapworth 16, 1924," a story that appeared in *The New Yorker* on June 19, 1965.

LITERARY GEOGRAPHY

What is the capital of Utopia in Thomas More's *Utopia* (1516)?
Amaurote.

Where was the Mermaid Tavern?
On Bread Street and Friday Street in London. It was a meeting place for poets and playwrights like Shakespeare, John Donne, Francis Beaumont, and John Fletcher.

What are the starting and ending points for the pilgrim in John Bunyan's *Pilgrim's Progress* (1678)?
Christian, the pilgrim, starts off in the City of Destruction and heads toward the Celestial City. On the

way he wanders into places like the Slough of De-
spond, the Valley of the Shadow of Death, and Vanity Fair.

Where is Brobdingnag?
In Jonathan Swift's *Gulliver's Travels* (1726), it is a
peninsula on the coast of California inhabited by giant plants, animals, and people.

Where is Grub Street?
The street that became synonymous with poor hack
writers was located in Moorfields, London. It no
longer exists.

What churchyard is the locale for Thomas Gray's "El-egy Written in a Country Churchyard" (1751)?
Probably Stoke Poges, where some of Gray's family
members were buried.

Where is Tintern Abbey?
The medieval abbey named in Wordsworth's 1798
poem is located in Monmouthshire, England, on the
Wye River. The poem is entitled "Lines Composed a
Few Miles above Tintern Abbey on Revisiting the
Banks of the Wye During a Tour, July 13, 1798."

In which polar region was the Ancient Mariner ma-rooned?
In the Antarctic, in Coleridge's 1798 poem "The Rime
of the Ancient Mariner."

On what corner was the Old Corner Bookstore?
It was located on the corner of Washington and

School streets in Boston. Founded in 1828, the store became a well-known gathering place for writers like Emerson, Hawthorne, Longfellow, and Whittier. Its owners were publishers William D. Ticknor and James T. Fields.

In Melville's *Moby-Dick* (1851), from where does Queequeg hail?
He is a cannibal and harpooner from the South Sea island of Kokovoko.

Where was Brook Farm?
The experiment in a utopian community was located in West Roxbury, Massachusetts. It was founded by transcendentalist George Ripley; its residents and visitors included Hawthorne, Emerson, and Margaret Fuller. It existed from 1841 to 1847.

What girls' school was the basis for the nightmarish Lowood in Charlotte Brontë's *Jane Eyre* (1847)?
The Clergy Daughters' School at Cowan Bridge, attended by four of the five Brontë sisters, including Charlotte.

Where did "The Charge of the Light Brigade" take place?
The six hundred British soldiers rode to their death at the hands of the Russian army at Balaclava in the Crimea, on October 25, 1854, in the 1854 poem by Alfred Lord Tennyson.

What was the name of Count Leo Tolstoy's estate?
Yasnaya Polyana, in central Russia.

What is the name of the fictitious region of rural England in which many of Thomas Hardy's novels are set?
Wessex. The first novel to use the setting was *Far from the Madding Crowd* (1874).

Where was Pearl S. Buck born?
Hillsboro, West Virginia, in 1892. But her missionary parents took her with them to China when she was a few months old, and she stayed there until 1933. *The Good Earth*, her novel of China, was published in 1931.

What was the name of the inn where H. G. Wells's *The Invisible Man* (1897) opens?
The Coach and Horses Inn in Iping, where Griffin, the invisible man, takes a room.

What was the former name of the Russian city called "Gorky"?
Nizhny Novgorod. It was renamed in 1932 in honor of its favorite son, playwright Maxim Gorky (1868–1936). "Maxim Gorky" itself was a pen name (meaning "most bitter") for Aleksei Maksimovich Peshkov. In 1991, the name reverted to Nizhny Novgorod.

What is the name of the place where Peter Pan takes the children?
While many early productions and Walt Disney called it "Never-Never Land," James M. Barrie's original version of *Peter Pan* (1904) refers to it as "Neverland."

Where was the Magic Mountain?
The sanatorium visited by Hans Castorp was located in Switzerland. *The Magic Mountain*, by Thomas Mann, was published in 1911.

Where is Spoon River?
Spoon River, site of the cemetery in poet Edgar Lee Masters's *Spoon River Anthology* (1915), is an area near Lewistown and Petersburg, Illinois, where Masters grew up. Many of the names of the deceased speakers in the anthology were taken from real tombstones in the Spoon River Cemetery.

Where is Winesburg, Ohio?
It was an imaginary small town in the 1919 novel by Sherwood Anderson.

Where was Sinclair Lewis's *Main Street* set?
The 1920 novel was set in a small town called Gopher Prairie. It may have been inspired by Lewis's hometown, Sauk Centre, Minnesota.

Where was Robert Frost born?
The "Voice of New England" was born in San Francisco in 1874. He moved to New England when he was ten.

What fictitious county in Mississippi is the locale for William Faulkner's *Sartoris* (1929), *The Sound and the Fury* (1929), *As I Lay Dying* (1930), and *Absalom, Absalom!* (1936)?
Yoknapatawpha County.

What is the name of the corrupt empire in George Orwell's *1984* (1949)?
Oceania, where main character Winston Smith lives. The superstate includes Britain; its archrivals are Eurasia and Eastasia.

Where is *The Bridge of San Luis Rey* (1927)?
The bridge near Lima, Peru, is a product of the imagination of the book's author, Thornton Wilder. Its collapse in 1714 sparks a study of destiny in the Pulitzer Prize–winning novel.

What part of the South is Eudora Welty from?
Jackson, Mississippi.

What town did novelist Thomas Wolfe (1900–38) call home?
The author of *You Can't Go Home Again* (1940) was born in Asheville, North Carolina.

Where is Shangri-La?
The fictional land is somewhere in Tibet, according to James Hilton's novel *Lost Horizon* (1933).

Where is Kilimanjaro, and does it snow there?
Mount Kilimanjaro is in Tanzania, Africa. At 19,340 feet, it is snow-capped year round. Ernest Hemingway's 1938 short story "The Snows of Kilimanjaro" is about a writer on safari in Africa.

Where in Africa was Isak Dinesen's farm?
The 4,000-acre coffee plantation was located in Kenya,

"at the foot of the Ngong Hills." It is described in *Out of Africa* (1938).

When did Paul Bowles, author of *The Sheltering Sky* (1949), live in Morocco?
Bowles has lived in Tangiers, Morocco, since 1947. He was born in New York in 1910.

In what part of Brooklyn is Bernard Malamud's novel *The Assistant* (1957) set?
In Malamud's own neighborhood of Flatbush during the Depression.

What suburb was home to the hero of *The Man in the Gray Flannel Suit* (1955)?
Tom Roth, the aspiring young executive in Sloan Wilson's novel, lived on Greentree Avenue in Westport, Connecticut.

Where is J. M. Coetzee's *Waiting for the Barbarians* (1980) set?
On the frontier of a mythical empire surrounded by barbarian tribes sometime in the twentieth century. Coetzee, a South African writer, took the title from a poem by Constantine P. Cavafy, "Waiting for the Barbarians."

Where in New York does Paul Auster's *New York Trilogy* begin?
City of Glass (1985), the first book in the trilogy, begins in Quinn's apartment on 107th Street off Broadway on Manhattan's Upper West Side.

LITERARY TERMS

What is an "aporia"?
It is a point of uncertainty or hesitation that is meant to convey irony. The speaker expresses indecision but does not really intend it: "I don't know what scares me more—your stupidity or your dishonesty."

What is the difference between an apothegm and an aphorism?
Very little. The two terms are often used synonymously for a short, pointed saying of known authorship. An apothegm, however, is especially short and usually witty. An example of an apothegm is attrib-

uted to Queen Elizabeth I: "Hope is a good breakfast, but it is a bad supper."

What is assonance?
Assonance is the use of similar vowel sounds (as in "grope" and "dome") to produce alliteration, or repetition of sounds. It is sometimes called "vowel rhyme."

What is consonance?
The use of similar consonant sounds (as in "leaves" and "lives") to produce alliteration.

What is the difference between blank verse and free verse?
Blank verse consists of unrhymed iambic pentameter lines; free verse is not defined by any set meter. Blank verse was introduced to England by Surrey in his translations of the *Aeneid* (1554).

What is catharsis?
The term was introduced by Aristotle in *The Poetics* (335–322 B.C.). He considered it a cleansing of the emotions of pity and fear, essential to tragedy.

What is concrete poetry?
An international avant-garde movement of the 1960s, concrete poetry attempted to offer a visual representation of its idea, often expressing itself through the poem's form on the page as well as through the meaning of the words. Practitioners included Eugen Gomringer.

What is a concrete universal?

It is the union in a literary work of a concrete, specific story or experience and abstract, universal truth. For example, Melville's *Moby-Dick* (1851) tells a specific story but represents universal meaning.

What is a courtesy book?

A book that outlines the education, conduct, and duties of a prince or courtier. Baldassare Castiglione's *Cortegiano* or *The Courtier* (1528) is an example.

What is the literal meaning of "dénouement"?

It is French for "untying." It refers to the final untangling of plot elements in a drama or narrative following a climax.

What is a *dinggedicht*?

Literally meaning "thing poem," a *dinggedicht* is a lyric poem that attempts to express the inner essence of an object. The poems in Rainer Maria Rilke's *Neue Gedichte* (1907) are examples.

What is an eclogue?

A pastoral poem in the form of a dialogue or soliloquy. The speakers are usually shepherds or their mistresses.

What is enjambment?

In poetry, a grammatical phrase that runs on from one line to the next without punctuation. It is the opposite of an "end-stopped" line, where the line ends with a grammatical pause (e.g., a period or comma).

What does "epiphany" mean?
In Greek mythology and literature, an epiphany occurs when a god or goddess reveals his or her true identity to a mortal. James Joyce adapted the term in his short stories to mean a moment of revelation. The Christian festival of Epiphany occurs on January 6, when Christ's divinity was revealed to the Magi.

Who invented the character Euphues?
John Lyly in *Euphues, the Anatomy of Wit* (1579). Euphues is a young Athenian man-about-town who gave his name to "euphuism": an elaborate style of discourse marked by alliteration, antitheses, and baroque figures. The style was much in fashion at the time—and much parodied.

Who first used the term "magic realism" as a literary definition?
American critic Alastair Reed used it to describe the fantastic fiction coming out of South America after World War II. The stories combined reportage and fantasy; authors included Carlos Fuentes, Julio Cortázar, Mario Vargas Llosa, and Gabriel García Marquez. The term has also been used to describe the work of writers in other countries, including Italo Calvino, Milan Kundera, and Salman Rushdie.

What is the meaning of "picaresque"?
Derived from the Spanish word for rogue, it refers to a literary genre that centers on the life of a criminal or ne'er-do-well. Picaresque stories usually unfold as a series of comic episodes. Examples can be found in Cervantes' *Novelas Ejemplares* (1613).

What is prosody?
The study of sound, rhythm, and meter in poetry.
(Meter is rhythm that occurs at regular intervals.)

What does it mean to "scan" a poem?
"Scansion" in poetry is the systematic analysis of patterns of stress or rhythm. To "scan" a poem is to analyze its rhythmic patterns, syllable by syllable; if the poem has a regular meter, "scansion" includes spotting the variations.

What is a Shakespearean sonnet?
It consists of three quatrains and a couplet, rhyming "abab cdcd efef gg." It is also referred to as the English sonnet.

What is a Spenserian stanza?
Invented by Edmund Spenser for *The Faerie Queene* (1590–96), the stanza has nine lines in iambic meter, with the first eight in pentameter and the ninth in hexameter, rhyming "ababbcbcc." Burns, Byron, Keats, and Shelley all used the Spenserian stanza at some point in their works.

What stresses would a word need to qualify as a spondee?
It would have to have two syllables, both accented, to qualify as this metrical foot. "Bookcase" and "heartbreak" are among the few examples.

What is a "spoonerism"?
It is a transposition of sounds, intended or otherwise, often with humorous effect. An example is "pouring

rain" for "roaring pain." The term is named for William Archibald Spooner (1844–1930), Dean and Warden of New College, Oxford, an allegedly gifted practitioner of the art.

What is "sprung rhythm"?
It is a type of rhythm used widely by Gerard Manley Hopkins, derived from the rhythm of nursery rhymes. It consisted in scanning by stresses alone, without any account of the number of syllables. In a line of poetry, it emphasized a stress on the first syllable of each foot.

Who introduced the term "stream of consciousness"?
William James in *Principles of Psychology* (1890) used the phrase to refer to the flow of thoughts and sensations, conscious and unconscious, in the human mind. The term came to refer to the fictional technique of representing a character's states in a free-flowing manner, often without conventional punctuation and syntax.

Who introduced the term "subtext"?
Twentieth-century French theater director Gaston Baty. He used it to refer to characters' motivations that are not explicitly stated in a play but can be understood.

THE
MIDDLE AGES

How many monsters does Beowulf kill?
Three—Grendel, Grendel's mother, and a dragon.
The Old English poem *Beowulf* is thought to date from
the eighth century.

What relation are Lancelot and Galahad?
Lancelot is Galahad's father. Both were knights of the
Round Table. Galahad is the only knight to peer into
the Holy Grail. Their adventures are told in, among
other places, Malory's *Le Morte d'Arthur* (1485).

Who were the Nine Worthies of medieval literature?
These illustrious men were three pagans (Hector of

Troy, Alexander the Great, and Julius Caesar); three Jews (Joshua, David, and Judas Maccabaeus); and three Christians (Arthur, Charlemagne, and Godfrey of Bouillon).

How does Roland die in the twelfth-century French epic *The Song of Roland*?

He dies at the battle of Roncesvalles when he blows on his horn to summon help from Charlemagne against the pagans. The action of blowing bursts his temples.

Who castrated Peter Abelard?

Abelard was castrated by order of the Canon Fulbert of Notre Dame in the twelfth century. Abelard (1079–1142), a philosopher and theologian, fell in love with his student Heloise (1101–64). They consummated their affair in 1118, had a son, and were secretly married. Heloise's uncle Fulbert learned of the affair and had Abelard castrated. Heloise became a nun and Abelard a monk. Their letters to one another still survive.

Who is the Brut in Layamon's *Brut*?

"Brut" is Brutus, the legendary founder of Britain, who is supposed to have been descended from the Trojans and to have traveled to the British Isles from Italy. The *Brut* by Layamon is a twelfth-century English translation and elaboration of Wace's *Roman de Brut* (1155), which is a French version of Geoffrey of Monmouth's Latin *History of the Kings of Britain* (c. 1135).

How old is Dante when he descends into the Inferno?
The year is 1300 and he is thirty-five—midway through the lifespan assigned by the Bible to humans (seventy years). Hence, the first words of Dante's *Inferno* (1321): "In the middle of the journey of our life I came to myself within a dark wood where the straight way was lost."

What other poems are in the manuscript that contains *Sir Gawain and the Green Knight*?
Four Middle English poems are written on the fourteenth-century "Cotton Nero A x" manuscript. All are in the dialect of the West Midlands. They are: *Sir Gawain and the Green Knight*, "Pearl," "Patience," and "Cleanness."

Who is Morgan le Fay?
She is a half-sister of King Arthur and a sorceress taught by Merlin. She appears, among other places, in the fourteenth-century poem *Sir Gawain and the Green Knight*.

When and where does Chaucer's *The Canterbury Tales* (c. 1387–1400) begin?
In April, probably 1387, at the Tabard Inn in Southwark, where a group of twenty-nine pilgrims has gathered to travel to the shrine of Thomas à Becket in Canterbury.

Who is Harry Bailly?
He is the host of the Tabard Inn. Bailly suggests

that the pilgrims to Canterbury tell each other tales to make the trip easier.

What is the significance of the title _The Second Shepherds' Play_?
This work is the second of two plays about shepherds in the Towneley cycle of medieval mystery plays. Both plays (late fourteenth–early fifteenth century) depict the shepherds' adoration of the infant Jesus. The second version is better known. It includes an episode about a thief named Mak who pretends a stolen sheep is a baby in a crib.

What is the Wife of Bath's Tale about?
In Chaucer's _Canterbury Tales_ (c. 1387–1400), the Wife of Bath tells the story of a knight who is condemned to death for rape, but who escapes punishment with the help of an ugly old witch. He then has to face the witch's demand that he marry her. The Wife of Bath's Tale, however, is best known for its long prologue, in which the Wife of Bath tells about her husbands and her views on marriage.

Did medieval mystics Margery Kempe and Julian of Norwich ever meet?
Yes, once, in 1413. Kempe stopped in on the recluse Julian during her travels. The visit is recorded in Kempe's spiritual autobiography _The Book of Margery Kempe_. Julian's single work is _A Revelation of Divine Love_ (c. 1393).

Who originated the term "courtly love"?
The term for a medieval code of ennobling love was

first introduced by critic Gaston Paris in 1883. There is some controversy about how widespread or fully developed the conception was in the Middle Ages. The medieval point of origin is traditionally seen as the poetry of the twelfth-century Provençal troubadours. In "courtly love," the knight served the lady, loved her passionately, and had a hard time fulfilling his desire—often because the lady was already married. Lancelot and Guinevere are the classic example of courtly lovers.

Whose death and burial is the last to be portrayed in Malory's *Le Morte d'Arthur* (1485)?
Lancelot's. King Arthur's death occurs several years—and several pages—earlier.

NONFICTION

What year was Augustine converted to Christianity?
In 387 A.D. He converted after hearing the preaching of St. Ambrose, bishop of Milan. The story is told in Augustine's *Confessions* (c. 400).

Who said, "I am myself the substance of my book, and there is no reason why you should waste your leisure on so frivolous and unrewarding a subject"?
Michel de Montaigne, in his note to the reader at the start of his *Essays* (1580).

What are the four "Idols of the Mind" in Bacon's *Novum Organum* (1620)?
The four tendencies to error, with their points of origin, are:

1. Idols of the Tribe—human nature
2. Idols of the Cave—individual character and circumstances
3. Idols of the Marketplace—society and language
4. Idols of the Theatre—false philosophical systems

What does the title *Areopagitica* mean?
Milton's essay in favor of unlicensed printing refers to the Areopagus, the council of ancient Athens that met on the hill of the same name to discuss public issues. *Areopagitica* (1644) means "things to be said before the Areopagus."

On what day does Samuel Pepys's *Diary* begin?
January 1, 1660, when Pepys (1633–1703) and his wife were living in poverty in Westminster. He later prospered as a government official. He ended his diary on May 31, 1669, fearing incorrectly that it was hurting his eyesight.

What is the first sentence?
"This morning (we lying lately in the garret) I rose, put on my suit with great shirts, having not lately worn any other clothes but them."

What did Swift propose in his pamphlet "A Modest Proposal" (1729)?
He satirically proposed that poor people raise their children to be slaughtered and sold as food to alleviate poverty in Ireland.

How long was *The Rambler* published?
Two years. Dr. Samuel Johnson published 208 issues of the semiweekly periodical from March 20, 1750, to March 14, 1752. All but five of the essays that compose *The Rambler* were written by Johnson.

How long did it take Samuel Johnson to write his *Dictionary*?
Eight years starting from 1747, when the idea was presented to him by a London bookseller, Dodsley, to 1755, when it was published. He received 575 pounds for his work.

When was Noah Webster's *American Dictionary of the English Language* first published?
In 1828.

What time span did David Hume's *History of Great Britain* (1754–62) cover?
It covered the years from Julius Caesar's invasion of Britain in the first century B.C. to the Glorious Revolution of 1688.

When did Gibbon get the idea to write *The History of the Decline and Fall of the Roman Empire* (1776–88)?
While he sat "musing amid the ruins of the Capitol" in Rome on October 15, 1764.

Who edited *L'Encyclopédie*?
Denis Diderot (1713–84), French philosopher. This compendium of knowledge was published in thirty-

five volumes between 1751 and 1776. It was meant to cover all aspects of life and embodied the rationalistic ideals of the Enlightenment. Contributors included Voltaire, Montesquieu, and Rousseau.

When did Blackstone write his histories of law?
The four-volume *Commentaries on the Laws of England* was published between 1765 and 1769.

How common was Thomas Paine's pamphlet "Common Sense"?
Considered to be the greatest literary influence on America's struggle for freedom, Paine's argument for freedom, anonymously published in January 1776, sold over 100,000 copies by March 1776. The colonial population at that time was around two million.

When did James Boswell and Samuel Johnson take their tour of the Hebrides?
Their seven-week journey to Scotland began on August 18, 1773. The journey is described in Boswell's *The Journal of a Tour to the Hebrides with Samuel Johnson, L.L.D.* (1785).

Who was George Washington's first biographer?
His name was Mason Locke Weems (1759–1825), an itinerant preacher better known as Parson Weems. His *History of the Life, Death, Virtues and Exploits of George Washington* (1800) is best known for the fictitious story of Washington's chopping down the cherry tree.

Who was the confessing party in *Confessions of an English Opium Eater* (1822)?
Thomas De Quincey, English critic (1785–1859).

How old was Karl Marx when *The Communist Manifesto* (1848) was published?
He was twenty-nine. He wrote the statement of revolutionary principles with fellow German socialist Friedrich Engels.

> **How old was Marx when the last volume of *Das Kapital* (1867–94) was published?**
> He was dead. Engels (1820–95) completed this systematic exposition of Communist theory from Marx's notes. Marx was born in 1818 and died in 1883.

Who was the Roget behind *Roget's Thesaurus*?
Peter Mark Roget (1779–1869), a British scholar and medical doctor. The book was first published in 1852.

Who wrote *Bulfinch's Mythology*?
It was written by Thomas Bulfinch (1796–1867). His works include *The Age of Fables* (1855) and *The Age of Chivalry* (1858).

To what work was John Henry Newman (1801–90) responding in *Apologia Pro Vita Sua* (1864)?
He was responding to a pamphlet by clergyman and novelist Charles Kingsley entitled "What, Then, Does Dr. Newman Mean?" (1864). The pamphlet followed an extended controversy between the Protestant

Kingsley and the Catholic convert Newman, in which Kingsley accused Newman of insincerity in his religious opinions. Newman's response is Latin for "A Defense of His Life."

According to Matthew Arnold (1822–88), which part of society made up the "Barbarians" and which the "Philistines"?
As discussed in many of his works, including *Culture and Anarchy* (1869), the aristocracy were the Barbarians, the commercial class the Philistines.

What cities are examined in Lincoln Steffens's *The Shame of the Cities*?
When the reporter created the 1904 book, he drew on several articles he had written for *McClure's* magazine in 1902 and 1903. Their titles read like a roster of American cities. They include:
    "Tweed Days in St. Louis"
    "The Shame of Minneapolis"
    "The Shamelessness of St. Louis"
    "Pittsburg [sic]: A City Ashamed"
    "Philadelphia: Corrupt and Corrupted"
    "Chicago: Half Free and Fighting On"
    "New York: Good Government to the Test"

What work introduces the relationship between the Dynamo and the Virgin?
In his autobiography, *The Education of Henry Adams* (1907), Adams contrasts the Dynamo (symbolizing modern life) and the Virgin (symbolizing the twelfth

century) while describing forty-foot dynamos exhibited at the Paris Exposition of 1900.

How many volumes does Sir James Frazer's *The Golden Bough* comprise?
The longest edition (1911–15) of Frazer's classic work on comparative mythology reached twelve volumes. An abridged edition was issued in 1922.

What are the *Ten Days that Shook the World*?
They are the days of the Russian Revolution of 1917, which brought an end to the imperial rule of the czars and replaced it with communism. The title refers to the 1919 eyewitness account of the revolution by American writer and sympathizer John Reed (1887–1920).

What dictionary was called the NED?
The New Oxford English Dictionary, now usually called the Oxford English Dictionary (OED). It was first published in 125 parts between 1884 and 1928; a 12-volume edition with supplements appeared in 1933. The NED has also been called the HED ("H" for "Historical"), Murray's dictionary (for editor James Murray), and the Society's dictionary (for the Philological Society).

How many books did Eleanor Roosevelt (1884–1962) write?
Five:
1. *This Is My Story* (1937)
2. *My Days* (1938)

3. *This I Remember* (1948)
4. *On My Own* (1958)
5. *The Autobiography of Eleanor Roosevelt* (1961)

That is three more than her husband, Franklin Delano Roosevelt (1882–1945), wrote:

1. *Looking Inward* (1933)
2. *On Our Way* (1934)

Mrs. Roosevelt also wrote a newspaper column, "My Day," and President Roosevelt's shorter writings are collected in *Papers and Addresses*.

When was the original *Oxford Companion to English Literature* published?
In 1932.

Who edited it?
Sir Paul Harvey.

Who was the Benét behind *Benét's Reader's Encyclopedia*?
William Rose Benét (1886–1950). The first edition appeared in 1948.

To what Native American tribe did Black Elk (1863–1950) belong?
The holy man/visionary who witnessed Custer's Last Stand, toured in Buffalo Bill's Wild West Show, and survived the massacre at Wounded Knee was a member of the Oglala Sioux. His oral autobiography *Black Elk Speaks* (1932) was recorded and edited by John Neihardt.

What were the names of the three tenant farm families described by James Agee and Walker Evans in *Let Us Now Praise Famous Men* (1941)?
They were the families of Fred and Sadie Ricketts, Thomas (Bud) and Ivy Woods, and George and Annie Mae Gudger. All lived in poverty in Alabama.

When was John Hersey's *Hiroshima* published?
The chronicle of the atomic bombing was published in *The New Yorker* and in book form in 1946, one year after the attack. Hersey (1914–   ) had been a World War II correspondent.

What part of New York City does the narrator call home in Alfred Kazin's memoir *A Walker in the City* (1951)?
The Brownsville section of Brooklyn.

How old was Primo Levi (1919–87) when he was sent to Auschwitz?
Twenty-four. The Italian Jewish writer tells the story of his captivity in Auschwitz from 1944 to 1945 in *Sequesto è un uomo* (tr. *If This Is a Man*, 1947). In the United States, the book is entitled *Survival in Auschwitz* (1958).

What kind of dog is Charley in *Travels with Charley*?
He is a poodle who accompanied John Steinbeck (1902–68) on his tour of the United States and was the title character in Steinbeck's 1962 book about the experience, *Travels with Charley, in Search of America*.

What writer did Jacqueline Kennedy hire to write a book about her husband's assassination?
She hired William Manchester to write the book that eventually became *The Death of a President* (1967).

For how many years did Anaïs Nin keep her diary?
From 1914, just before coming to the United States from Spain, until her death in 1977. The French-born avant-garde writer achieved her greatest fame when *The Diary of Anaïs Nin 1931–1966* was published in seven volumes from 1966 to 1980.

Who are the Boys of Summer that Roger Kahn wrote about in *The Boys of Summer* (1971)?
They are the lineup and pitchers of the 1950s Brooklyn Dodgers and include:
> Joe Black
> Roy Campanella
> Billy Cox
> Carl Erskine
> Carl Furillo
> Gil Hodges
> Clem Labine
> Andy Pafko
> Pee Wee Reese
> Jackie Robinson
> Preacher Roe
> George Shuba
> Duke Snider

How many books of autobiography has Maya Angelou (1928–) written?
Five:
1. *I Know Why the Caged Bird Sings* (1969)
2. *Gather Together in My Name* (1974)
3. *Singin' and Swingin' and Gettin' Merry Like Christmas* (1976)
4. *The Heart of a Woman* (1981)
5. *All God's Children Need Travelling Shoes* (1986)

In the 1987 memoir by Geoffrey Wolff, who is the "Duke of Deception"?
He is Wolff's father, Arthur Samuels Wolff. He was also known by the false names, Saunders Ansell-Wolff III and Arthur Saunders Wolff III. His nickname was "Duke."

To what work does the title of M. Scott Peck's *The Road Less Traveled* (1979) allude?
Robert Frost's poem "The Road Not Taken" (1915, 1916). The phrase used by Peck, however, occurs nowhere in the poem. The closest approximation is: "Two roads diverged in a wood, and I—/I took the one less traveled by,/And that has made all the difference."

Where did Annie Dillard spend the childhood she writes about in her memoir *An American Childhood* (1987)?
Dillard (1945–) grew up in Pittsburgh, Pennsylvania.

OMNIBUS

What classical work described a trip to the moon?
The True History, by Lucian of Samosata (c. 125–200
A.D.), a Greek writer of prose satires. Among writers
influenced by Lucian were Jonathan Swift in *Gulliver's Travels*.

How many suras are in the Koran?
There are 114 suras, or chapters, generally arranged
from longest to shortest.

**Into how many languages has the Bible been trans-
lated?**
About 1,735.

What are the chances of a monkey with a typewriter composing *Hamlet*?
The odds have been calculated as 1 in $35^{200,000}$.

For whom is the Bodleian Library named?
The library at Oxford University was named for its founder Sir Thomas Bodley (1545–1613), scholar and diplomat. The Bodleian Library opened in 1602.

What was Spinoza's nationality?
Philosopher Baruch (or Benedict) Spinoza (1632–77) was born in Amsterdam of Portuguese Jewish parents.

How do you pronounce diarist Samuel Pepys's last name?
"Peeps" or "peppis."

Does a dactyl have anything to do with a pterodactyl?
Both words are derived from the Greek word for "finger." A dactyl is a metrical foot consisting of one long or stressed syllable, followed by two short or unstressed ones. "Stroking him tenderly" is a short dactylic line. The word "dactyl" refers to the three joints of the finger. The word "pterodactyl," referring to a prehistoric flying reptile, means "winged finger."

Which people preferred opening which end of their eggs in Jonathan Swift's *Gulliver's Travels* (1726)?
The people of Lilliput, less than six inches high, open their eggs at the little end. Their archenemies, the

people of the nearby island of Blefuscu, open their eggs at the big end. They are known as "Big-Enders." Lilliput is in the Indian Ocean southwest of Sumatra.

Which author named Fielding wrote the novel *The Adventures of David Simple* (1744)?
Sarah Fielding, Henry's younger sister. The novel was a big success and spawned two sequels.

Who wrote the following works about castles?
1. *The Castle of Perseverance*—anonymous, morality play, c. 1405–25
2. *The Castle of Indolence*—James Thomson, poem, 1748
3. *The Castle of Otranto*—Horace Walpole, novel, 1764
4. *Castle Dangerous*—Walter Scott, novel, 1832
5. *Castle Richmond*—Anthony Trollope, novel, 1860

How does Samuel Johnson's *A Dictionary of the English Language* (1747–55) define man and woman?
Man:
1. Human being.
2. Not a woman.
3. Not a boy.
4. A servant; an attendant; a dependent.
5. A word of familiarity bordering on contempt.
6. It is used in a loose signification like the French *un*, one, any one.
7. One of uncommon qualifications.

8. A human being qualified in any particular manner.
9. Individual.
10. Not a beast.
11. Wealthy or independent.
12. When a person is not in his senses, we say, he is not his own *man*.
13. A moveable piece at chess or draughts.
14. Man of war. A ship of war.

Woman:
1. The female of the human race.
2. A female attendant on a person of rank.

How did Ambrose Bierce define "man" in *The Devil's Dictionary* (1911)?
"An animal so lost in rapturous contemplation of what he thinks he is as to overlook what he indubitably ought to be. His chief occupation is extermination of other animals and his own species, which, however, multiplies with such insistent rapidity as to infest the whole habitable earth and Canada."

Who wrote "A Dissertation on Roast Pig"?
Charles Lamb in his *Essays of Elia* (1823, 1833).

What Mary Shelley novel is set in the future?
The Last Man (1826). Set in the twenty-first century, it depicts England as a republic and describes the destruction of humanity by plague.

What were the real names of poets Currer, Ellis, and Acton Bell?
Charlotte, Emily, and Anne Brontë. Their *Poems by Currer, Ellis, and Acton Bell* appeared in 1846. Currer Bell was also the pseudonym under which Charlotte's *Jane Eyre* (1847) was first published.

Is there a hyphen in the title of Herman Melville's *Moby-Dick* (1851)?
Yes, but it is often dropped.

Who wrote the play that Lincoln was watching when he was assassinated?
The author of *Our American Cousin* (1858) was Tom Taylor. He was an editor of the English magazine *Punch*.

Who is the Dewey behind the Dewey decimal system?
Melvil Dewey invented the system in 1876. The system divides books into ten main categories of knowledge, using numbers that range from 000 to 999. Subcategories are assigned decimal numbers.

Where are erotic books stored at the Library of Congress?
They are gathered at the library in a grouping called the Delta Collection.

What is the difference between Beatrice Potter (1858–1943) and Beatrix Potter (1866–1943)?
Beatrice Potter was the maiden name of Beatrice Webb, the wife of Sidney Webb. The Webbs were

leading cultural figures at the end of the nineteenth century, particularly active in the Fabian Society. Beatrix Potter was the author of several children's books, including *The Tale of Peter Rabbit* (1902). She lived quietly on a farm with her husband, William Heelis.

When did "The Protocols of the Elders of Zion" first appear?

The antisemitic forgery first appeared in a St. Petersburg newspaper in 1903. It purported to document the conspiracy of Judaism to take over the world. It may have been written by Czar Nicholas II's secret police.

Was there a Fannie Farmer?

She was cooking instructor and administrator Fannie Merritt Farmer (1857–1915) and the author of *The Boston Cooking School Cookbook* (1896). As principal of the Boston Cooking School and creator of Miss Farmer's School of Cookery, she published five other cookbooks, including *Food and Cookery for the Sick and Convalescent* (1904) and the *New Book of Cookery* (1912).

Who wrote "Paul Bunyan and His Big Blue Ox"?

The tale first appeared as an advertising pamphlet from the Red River Lumber Company in 1914, credited to W. B. Laughead. The legends about Paul Bunyan can be traced to a French-Canadian logger in the 1830s named Paul Bunyon.

Who wrote *20,000 Leagues Under the Sea, or, David Copperfield?*

Humorist Robert Benchley published this collection of essays in 1928.

What relation were authors George Du Maurier and Daphne Du Maurier?
George, author of *Trilby* (1894) and *Peter Ibbetson* (1891), was the grandfather of Daphne, author of *Rebecca* (1938).

What is "bababadalgharaghtakamminarronnkonn-bronntonnerronntuonnthunntrovarrhounawn-skawntoohoohoordenenthurnuk!"?
This 100-letter word for the symbolic thunderclap representing the fall of Adam and Eve appears on the first page of James Joyce's *Finnegans Wake* (1939).

What was Alice B. Toklas's nickname?
Pussy.

What is novelist Ralph Ellison's middle name?
Waldo.

Who was "Old Possum"?
The nickname "Old Possum" was given to T. S. Eliot by Ezra Pound; Eliot frequently signed his name that way on letters. The name was used in *Old Possum's Book of Practical Cats* (1939), the basis for the Broadway musical *Cats*.

What novels did Gypsy Rose Lee write?
The stripper/stage performer wrote two mysteries: *The G-String Murders* in 1941 and *Mother Finds a Body* in 1942. Finding the writing profession not lucrative enough, she returned to her earlier career.

Was Vachel Lindsay male or female?
The Kentucky-born poet of the early twentieth century was male.

Countee Cullen?
The poet of the Harlem Renaissance was male.

Julian of Norwich?
The medieval mystic was female.

What is the name of the other streetcar in Tennessee Williams's play *A Streetcar Named Desire* (1947)?
"Cemetery" and "Desire" are the two streetcars running on the same track.

When could you have attended a course taught by Vladimir Nabokov?
From 1948 to 1959 at Cornell. A professor of Russian literature, Nabokov was able to retire, thanks to the success of the bestselling *Lolita* (1955).

What is an orc?
It depends on the author you are reading. Renaissance authors Ludovico Ariosto, John Milton, Michael Drayton, and others used the term to describe a sea monster, from Latin *orca*, or whale. William Blake gave the name "Orc" to his personification of rebellion and anarchy in poems such as "America: A Prophecy" (1793). And J. R. R. Tolkien, in *The Lord of the Rings* (1954–55), used the name for a species of evil, goblinlike creatures.

How many _Dune_ novels did Frank Herbert write?
Six:
1. _Dune_ (1965)
2. _Dune Messiah_ (1969)
3. _Children of Dune_ (1976)
4. _God Emperor of Dune_ (1981)
5. _Heretics of Dune_ (1984)
6. _Chapterhouse: Dune_ (1985)

What is the alien planet visited by Billy Pilgrim in Kurt Vonnegut's _Slaughterhouse-Five_ (1969)?
Tralfamadore, 446,120,000,000,000,000 miles from Earth.

Who is married in the wedding that opens Mario Puzo's _The Godfather_ (1969)?
Don Vito Corleone's daughter Constanzia (Connie) and Carlo Rizzi. The wedding takes place on the last Saturday in August, 1945, at the Don's house on Long Island.

How do you spell the first name of the author of _The Shining_ (1977)?
His name is Stephen, not Steven, King.

How do you spell the last name of the author of _Communion_ (1988)?
His name is Whitley Strieber (not Streiber). _Communion_ is his supposedly nonfiction account of an encounter with extraterrestrials.

What is the name of the title character in Leon Rooke's *Shakespeare's Dog* (1983)?
Hooker.

From what country does Mario Vargas Llosa hail?
Peru.

Jorge Luis Borges?
Argentina.

Gabriel Garcia Marquez?
Colombia.

Federico García Lorca?
Spain.

Miguel de Unamuno?
Spain.

Who founded PEN?
English novelist and playwright John Galsworthy (*The Forsyte Saga*) founded Poets, Playwrights, Essayists, Editors, and Novelists (PEN) in London in 1921. It is a worldwide association to preserve international ties among writers. The American branch of PEN was opened in 1923.

How many exclamation points are there in the text of Tom Wolfe's novel *The Bonfire of the Vanities* (1987)?
Wolfe's hyperbolic satire of modern Manhattan contains 2,343 exclamation points.

What books do Americans consider most influential in their lives?
According to a 1991 survey of Book-of-the-Month Club readers, the five most influential books are:
1. The Bible.
2. *Atlas Shrugged* by Ayn Rand.
3. *The Road Less Traveled* by M. Scott Peck.
4. *To Kill a Mockingbird* by Harper Lee.
5. *The Lord of the Rings* by J. R. R. Tolkien.

PERIODICALS

Who did the tattling in *The Tatler*?
Richard Steele and Joseph Addison's periodical appeared three times a week from 1709 to 1711. The pseudonymous editor was Isaac Bickerstaff.

Who did the spectating in *The Spectator* (1711–12)?
Addison and Steele's periodical *The Spectator* was named for a character named Sir Roger de Coverley. Sir Roger was a good-hearted country squire who, as a member of the fictitious Spectator Club, commented on the notion of the English gentleman in the reign of Queen Anne.

How long was *Poor Richard's Almanack* published?
Benjamin Franklin published it in Philadelphia from 1733 to 1758. After 1748, the almanac was called *Poor Richard Improved*. Franklin sold it in 1758, but it continued to be published until 1796.

In what periodical was Edgar Allan Poe's poem "The Raven" first published?
The New York *Evening Mirror*, on January 29, 1845.

When did *Harper's Magazine* begin publication?
Founded in 1850 as *Harper's New Monthly Magazine*, the literary periodical was edited by William Dean Howells (1837–1920). After World War I, the magazine began to print political and social articles. In 1925 it was renamed *Harper's Magazine*.

Who created *The New York Times* slogan "All the news that's fit to print"?
Newspaperman Adolph Simon Ochs (1858–1935), who purchased *The New York Times* at the turn of the century.

When was *Poetry* magazine founded?
The forum for works by many of the most influential American poets of the first part of the twentieth century was founded in Chicago in 1912 by Harriet Monroe.

When was the magazine *The Egoist* published?
In London from 1914 until 1919. Originally called *The New Free Woman: An Individualist Review*, it ran

articles on modern poetry and the arts. It was founded by Harriet Shaw Weaver and Dora Marsden and supported by writers like Ezra Pound and T. S. Eliot. Joyce's *Portrait of the Artist as a Young Man* first appeared there in 1914–15.

According to H. L. Mencken, when was the first American bathtub installed?

In an article entitled "A Neglected Anniversary," published on December 28, 1917, in the *New York Evening Mail*, Mencken claimed the first American bathtub was installed on December 20, 1842, "and, for all I know to the contrary, it may be still in existence and in use." The article was cited often thereafter as an accurate reference source; Mencken finally admitted he made it up.

At its height, how large was the publishing empire created by William Randolph Hearst?

It included eighteen newspapers across the country, and nine magazines, including *The San Francisco Daily Examiner* and *Good Housekeeping*.

When was *Reader's Digest* first published?

February 1922. In 1941, its circulation was 4 million; today it is 28 million.

Who is the dandy with the monocle associated with *The New Yorker*?

Eustace Tilley, drawn by Rea Irvin for the magazine's first cover in 1925.

When was James Thurber on the staff of *The New Yorker*?

Thurber (1894–1961) was on staff at the magazine from 1927 to 1933. He remained a regular contributor afterward.

When did William Shawn become editor of *The New Yorker*?

On January 21, 1952. He succeeded Harold Ross, who founded the magazine in 1925. In 1987, Robert Gottlieb became the magazine's editor. Tina Brown took over in 1992.

Who founded *The Kenyon Review*?

Poet and professor John Crowe Ransom, while teaching at Kenyon in 1939.

What magazine rejected the original version of James Agee and Walker Evans's *Let Us Now Praise Famous Men* (1941)?

Their 1936 account of tenant farm families in the South was commissioned by *Fortune* magazine but rejected. Houghton Mifflin eventually published an expanded version.

When did Norman Cousins edit *The Saturday Review*?

From 1942 to 1971. Founded in 1924 as a literary magazine, the periodical was expanded under Cousins to include the other arts and international affairs. In 1952, the magazine's name was changed from *The Saturday Review of Literature* to *The Saturday Review*.

What are the top three best-selling magazines in the United States?

In 1990, with circulation, they were:

1. *NRTA/AARP Bulletin*—22,103,887
2. *Reader's Digest*—16,264,547
3. *TV Guide*—15,604,267

What are the top three daily newspapers in the United States?

In 1990, with circulation, they were:

1. *The Wall Street Journal*—1,857,131
2. *USA Today*—1,347,450
3. *The Los Angeles Times*—1,196,323

POETRY

How many syllables are in a haiku?
This highly stylized form of poetry consists of three unrhymed lines of five, seven, and five syllables respectively—a total of seventeen syllables.

Who was Colin Clout?
Clout the shepherd was Spenser's alter ego in *The Shepheardes Calendar* (1579), a series of twelve eclogues, one for each month of the year. Clout was in love with the beautiful Rosalind. He reappears in Spenser's *Colin Clouts Come Home Againe* (1595) and *The Faerie Queene* (1590–96).

What is an "epithalamium"?
A poem or song celebrating marriage. The form was popular in the Renaissance. The most famous example is Edmund Spenser's "Epithalamion" (1595).

> **For whose wedding did Spenser write "Epithalamion"?**
> His own, to Elizabeth Boyle, in 1594.

Of Hero and Leander, which is the male, which the female?
In the erotic unfinished poem of 1598 by Christopher Marlowe, Leander is the male who pursues Hero, the female. The pursuit leads eventually to physical union.

In which Christmas season did Milton write "On the Morning of Christ's Nativity"?
Christmas 1629.

How many poets have written poems beginning, "Come live with me and be my love"?
At least three. Christopher Marlowe used it in the 1600 poem "The Passionate Shepherd to His Love"; John Donne in the 1612 poem "The Bait"; and C. Day Lewis in the 1935 poem "Song."

What items sat on the main character's dressing table in "The Rape of the Lock" by Alexander Pope (1688–1744)?
Among the items on Belinda's table in the 1714 poem

are the following: "puffs, patches, powders, Bibles and billets-doux."

What poet said "Let Newton be"?
Alexander Pope, in the following couplet:
"Nature, and Nature's laws, lay hid in night.
God cried, 'Let Newton be!', and all was light."

Who forged a group of poems attributed to the legendary Gaelic warrior Ossian?
Scottish writer James Macpherson from 1760 to 1763. He claimed to have "discovered" the poems in ancient manuscripts.

Who were the Lake poets?
They were a group of Romantic poets who lived in the Lake District of England in the late eighteenth and early nineteenth centuries. They included William Wordsworth, Samuel Taylor Coleridge, and Robert Southey.

To what baby is Coleridge's lyric poem "Frost at Midnight" (1798) addressed?
His son Hartley.

How old was William Cullen Bryant (1794–1878) when he wrote the poem "Thanatopsis"?
He was sixteen. The poem was not published until he was in his twenties, in 1817.

What work is the basis for Keats's poem "Lamia"?
The 1819–20 poem about the serpent Lamia, who is

turned into a woman, is derived from the 1621 work *Anatomy of Melancholy* by Robert Burton.

What is the line that follows "I wandered lonely as a cloud"?

"That floats on high o'er vales and hills." Wordsworth's poem "I Wandered Lonely as a Cloud" was first published in 1807.

Who unbinds Prometheus in Shelley's *Prometheus Unbound* (1820)?

Hercules releases Prometheus from the rock to which he is chained as a punishment for defying Jupiter.

For whom did Percy Bysshe Shelley write "Adonais"?

The poem, written in 1821, is an elegy to John Keats, who died the same year.

Whose attack on poetry sparked Shelley's "Defense of Poetry" (1821)?

Thomas Love Peacock. Peacock's satirical essay "The Four Ages of Poetry" (1820) belittled the value of poetry.

When were Byron's memoirs burned?

On May 17, 1824, in the London home of publisher John Murray. The manuscript was thought to be deleterious to the deceased poet's reputation. Among those present at the burning was a representative for Lady Byron.

What poems did William Wordsworth write as poet laureate (1843–50)?
He did not produce any poetry during this time. Other poets were dismayed that Wordsworth accepted the position; Robert Browning wrote the poem "The Lost Leader" (1843) in response.

Who is Empedocles and what is he doing on Etna in Matthew Arnold's poem "Empedocles on Etna" (1852)?
Empedocles was a Greek philosopher of the fifth century B.C. He was supposed to have committed suicide by throwing himself into the crater of Mount Etna. The poem depicts his dialogue with his friend Pausanius at the edge of the crater, as Pausanias tries unsuccessfully to convince him not to jump.

Who wrote, "Tell me not in mournful numbers/Life is but an empty dream"?
Henry Wadsworth Longfellow in the poem "A Psalm of Life" (1839).

In what meter is Longfellow's "The Song of Hiawatha" (1855) written?
Unrhymed trochaic tetrameter. The meter is also found in the Finnish epic *Kalevala*. A trochee is a foot of one stressed and one unstressed syllable; a tetrameter line is four feet: "By the shore of Gitche Gumee."

How many editions did *Leaves of Grass* go through during Walt Whitman's (1819–92) lifetime?
The often revised poem went through nine editions after its initial publication in 1855.

Who was the real-life painter behind Browning's poem "Fra Lippo Lippi" (1855)?
Filippo Lippi (c. 1406–69), a Carmelite monk and a painter of the Florentine school. Browning based his dramatic monologue about Lippi on a passage in Vasari's *Lives of the Painters*.

Who wrote the poem "The Wreck of the Hesperus" (1841)?
Henry Wadsworth Longfellow.

> **Who wrote the poem "The Wreck of the Deutschland" (1875)?**
> Gerard Manley Hopkins.

When did Gerard Manley Hopkins burn his poems?
Hopkins (1844–89) burned his poems in 1868, on resolving to become a Jesuit. He had converted from Anglicanism to Roman Catholicism in 1866. However, he had sent copies to fellow poet Robert Bridges and went on writing poetry throughout his life, so the burning was only symbolic.

> **How long after his death were Hopkins's poems first published?**
> The first substantial edition of his poetry was published by Bridges in 1918—twenty-nine years after Hopkins's death.

Whose death was the occasion of Walt Whitman's "When Lilacs Last in the Dooryard Bloom'd" (1865–66)?
Abraham Lincoln's.

What were the slithy toves doing in the first stanza of Lewis Carroll's "Jabberwocky" (1871)?
"Twas brillig, and the slithy toves
Did gyre and gimble in the wabe;"

How many of Emily Dickinson's poems were published during her lifetime (1830–86)?
Seven. She wrote over 1,500.

Who wrote "Casey at the Bat"?
The long-lived poem was written by Ernest Lawrence Thayer and first published in *The San Francisco Examiner* on June 3, 1888.

Who wrote that poem about the purple cow?
Gelett Frank Burgess (1866–1951). Later, in the *Burgess Nonsense Book* (1914), he wrote:
"Ah, yes! I wrote the 'Purple Cow'—
I'm sorry, now, I wrote it!
But I can tell you anyhow,
I'll kill you if you quote it!"

What poem contains the line "A terrible beauty is born"?
Yeats's "Easter 1916" (1916).

When was Marianne Moore a librarian at the New York Public Library?
Between 1921 and 1925, during which time two volumes of her poetry were published: *Poems* (1921) and *Observations* (1924).

To whom is T. S. Eliot's poem *The Waste Land* (1922) dedicated?
Ezra Pound. The poem was radically altered and edited by Pound, whom Eliot describes in his dedication as *"il miglior fabbro,"* the better craftsman.

What are the five parts of the poem?
"The Burial of the Dead," "A Game of Chess," "The Fire Sermon," "Death by Water," and "What the Thunder Said."

What are the four poems that comprise Eliot's *Four Quartets*?
The poems in the 1943 collection are: "Burnt Norton," "East Coker," "The Dry Salvages," and "Little Gidding." The poems had been published separately between 1935 and 1942.

Did William Carlos Williams live in Paterson, New Jersey?
No. Aside from attending school in New York City, Philadelphia, Switzerland, and Germany, he lived, wrote, and practiced medicine in his hometown, Rutherford, New Jersey.

How many words are in Williams's poem "The Red Wheelbarrow" (1923)?
Sixteen, if you count "wheel/barrow" and "rain/water" as two words each.

Which poet was born first: Amy Lowell, James Russell Lowell, or Robert Lowell?
James Russell (1819–92) was born first, Amy (1874–

1925) second, and Robert (1917–77) third. All were from New England.

Who wrote "The Night Before the Night Before Christmas"?
Randall Jarrell (1914–65), alluding to Clement Moore's "A Visit from St. Nicholas" (1823).

When did the "New York School" of poets flourish?
The New York School were a group of poets based in New York City during the late 1950s and early 1960s. Their poetry tended to be cosmopolitan, witty, hallucinatory, and influenced by abstract painting. The school had its origins at Harvard, where poets John Ashbery, Frank O'Hara, and Kenneth Koch met as students before migrating to New York.

Who started the Black Mountain School of poetry?
Charles Olson (1910–70), in the early 1950s, at experimental Black Mountain College, in Asheville, North Carolina. Some of Olson's students included poets Robert Creeley and Denise Levertov.

What are the "dream songs"?
They are a series of 432 poems by John Berryman (1914–72) about "Henry," a man who "has suffered a terrible loss." Berryman began writing them in 1955, and worked on them until his death.

What poet read at John Kennedy's inauguration in 1961?
Robert Frost, who tried to read a composition he had

written for the occasion. The sunlight was too dazzling for him to see the words, so he recited another of his poems, "Dedication," which he dedicated to "the President-elect John Finley."

What poem did Marianne Moore and Muhammad Ali write together?
It was called "A Poem on the Annihilation of Ernie Terrell," and was written on the occasion of an upcoming fight between Terrell and Ali (then Cassius Clay) in 1967. The poem was published in newspapers through the Associated Press.

How many r's are in the names of poets John Berryman and John Ashbery?
There are two r's in "Berryman," one in "Ashbery."

Which one killed himself?
John Berryman, in 1972.

POPULAR
LITERATURE

Who is credited with originating "dime novels"?
Edward Zane Carroll Judson, whose pen name was
Ned Buntline. Judson was the author of over 400 dime
novels, including *The Scouts of the Plains* (1872).

Was there a Deadwood Dick?
Yes. This was the nickname of English-born Richard
W. Clarke (1845–1930), a frontier personality in South
Dakota, who guarded gold shipments and did battle
with Indians. Edward L. Wheeler wrote a popular
series of dime novels about Deadwood Dick's education.

Who wrote *Ben-Hur?*
Lewis (Lew) Wallace in 1880. The complete title of the book is *Ben-Hur: A Tale of the Christ.* A Union general and politician, Wallace served as governor of New Mexico and Indiana.

Did Arthur Conan Doyle write any other books besides those featuring Sherlock Holmes?
Yes, more than ten others, including science fiction and historical fiction. They include: *Micah Clarke* (1889), *The White Company* (1891), and *The Lost World* (1912).

What book introduced Svengali?
The sinister hypnotist-musician Svengali was introduced by George Du Maurier in his novel *Trilby* (1894). Svengali uses mesmerism to make Trilby O'Ferrall a great singer, but she loses her voice when he dies of a heart attack.

Who wrote *Quo Vadis?*
The novel of Nero's Rome was published by Polish writer Henryk Sienkiewicz in 1895.

Who wrote *Little Black Sambo?*
British author Helen Bannerman wrote and illustrated the popular and now controversial story in 1899; it was followed by *Little Black Mingo* (1901); *Little Black Quibba* (1902); *Little Black Quasha* (1908); and *Little Black Bobtail* (1910).

Who wrote *The Virginian?*
The Virginian: A Horseman of the Plains, the book that

set the mold for the Western novel, was written in 1902 by Owen Wister.

What was Kathleen Winsor's follow-up to *Forever Amber*?
It was *Wanderers East, Wanderers West*, about frontier days in Montana, published nearly twenty years after her best-selling 1945 novel.

What was Ellery Queen's real name?
The two authors who created Ellery Queen were Frederic Dannay (1905–82) and Manfred Lee (1905–71). They began writing mysteries under their joint pseudonym in 1929, with *The Roman Hat Mystery*.

Which detective novels by Dorothy L. Sayers do not feature detective Lord Peter Wimsey?
Only one—*The Documents in the Case* (1930), written with Robert Eustace.

What was the nationality of Kahlil Gibran?
The author of *The Prophet* (1923) and *The Garden of the Prophet* (1934) was Lebanese. He was born in 1883 and died in 1931.

Who wrote the novel *The African Queen* (1935)?
C. S. Forester.

In the John O'Hara novel of the same name, whose phone number begins with Butterfield 8?
Among others at this Park Avenue telephone ex-

change is Gloria Wandrous, girl-about-town and central character. *Butterfield 8* was published in 1935.

How many copies of Margaret Mitchell's *Gone With the Wind* (1936) are sold every year?
About 250,000 copies are sold annually. The sales total so far is about 28 million copies.

Who was the hobbit-hero of Tolkien's *The Hobbit* (1937)?
Bilbo Baggins.

> **Who was the hobbit-hero of the sequel, *The Lord of the Rings* (1954–55)?**
> Bilbo's nephew, Frodo Baggins.

What does the "M" in James M. Cain (1892–1977) stand for?
Mallahan. The novelist was the author of *The Postman Always Rings Twice* (1934) and *Mildred Pierce* (1941).

What was the name of Sam Spade's partner in Dashiell Hammett's *The Maltese Falcon* (1930)?
Miles Archer. He was killed early in the novel by Brigid O'Shaughnessey.

Who was "The Continental Op"?
He was the unnamed detective from the Continental Detective Agency who ran the investigation of corruption in Dashiell Hammett's *Red Harvest* (1929).

How many works by Daphne Du Maurier were made into movies by Alfred Hitchcock?

Three:
1. *Jamaica Inn* (novel, 1936; filmed 1939)
2. *Rebecca* (novel, 1938; filmed 1940)
3. *The Birds* (short story, filmed 1963)

What is the profession of the title character in *What Makes Sammy Run*?

Sammy Glick is a New York–born Hollywood movie mogul in the 1941 novel by Budd Schulberg.

Who is the captain and what is the name of the ship in *Mister Roberts*?

Captain Morton was the martinet leader of the USS *Reluctant* in the 1946 novel by Thomas Heggen. Heggen and Joshua Logan adapted it for the stage; the story was filmed in 1955. Ensign Pulver disposes of the captain's palm tree in all three versions.

What was James Michener's first book?

A collection of short stories, *Tales of the South Pacific*, which was published in 1947 and won the Pulitzer Prize. Before he became a full-time writer, Michener was a textbook editor at Macmillan.

What pseudonyms did Isaac Asimov use?

The prolific author (1920–92) wrote books as George E. Dale, Dr. A, and Paul French.

On what town is *Peyton Place* (1956) based?

Gilmantown, New Hampshire. The author of *Peyton Place*, Grace Metalious, is buried there.

What was the name of the book Peyton Place resident Alison Mackenzie wrote that caused such a stir?
It was called *Samuel's Castle,* and it appeared in the sequel to *Peyton Place* (1956), *Return to Peyton Place* (1959).

What previously published books comprise *The Once and Future King* (1958)?
The book by T. H. White is made of revised versions of four previously published books: *The Sword in the Stone* (1939), *The Witch in the Wood* (1940), *The Ill-Made Knight* (1941), and *The Candle in the Wind* (1958).

What is the name of the religious order that preserves scientific books after a nuclear holocaust in Walter M. Miller, Jr.'s *A Canticle for Leibowitz* (1959)?
The Order of Albertus Magnus. The Leibowitz of the title was the former technician who formed the order to protect scientific knowledge from angry holocaust survivors.

What book did Raymond Chandler (1888–1959) leave unfinished when he died?
The Poodle Springs Story. It was completed by Robert Parker as *Poodle Springs* in 1989.

What colors have been mentioned in the titles of the Travis McGee series by John D. MacDonald (1916–86)?
The titles of MacDonald's mystery series (*Bright Orange for the Shroud, Cinnamon Skin*, etc.) all contain colors. Colors mentioned include the following:

orange	silver
cinnamon	lavender
amber	pink
gold	yellow
blue	gray
lemon	purple
indigo	red
copper	scarlet
crimson	tan
brown	turquoise
green	

What is "the cold" in John le Carré's *The Spy Who Came in from the Cold* (1963)?
The undercover life of being a spy. The main character, Alec Leamas, British double agent in East Germany, finally comes in from the cold by allowing himself to be shot at the Berlin Wall.

What is the real name of the planet known as Dune in Frank Herbert's *Dune* (1965)?
Arrakis.

> **What is the homeworld of Paul Atreides (Muad'Dib)?**
> Caladan.

> **What is the homeworld of the evil Baron Harkonnen, archrival of the Atreides?**
> Giedi Prime.

What were the dolls in *Valley of the Dolls*?
In Jacqueline Susann's 1966 novel, the "dolls" were the pills taken by the aspiring Hollywood actresses.

How many people wrote *Naked Came the Stranger*?
Twenty writers each contributed a chapter to the 1969 novel, published under the name Penelope Ashe.

What is the epigraph at the start of Mario Puzo's *The Godfather* (1969)?
"Behind every great fortune there is a crime" (Balzac).

Under what pseudonym does Gore Vidal write mystery stories?
Edgar Box.

Who is the leader of the rabbit warren in Richard Adams's *Watership Down* (1972)?
Hazel, leader of the warren called Watership Down. His archenemy is General Woundwort, leader of the neighboring Efrata Warren.

What was the name of the marathon man in William Goldman's *Marathon Man* (1974)?
Thomas Babington Levy, or "Babe."

For what president did Peter Benchley work before becoming a novelist?
He was a speechwriter for President Lyndon Johnson before writing the best-selling novel *Jaws* (1974).

What town does Carrie devastate on the night of her prom in Stephen King's *Carrie* (1974)?
The telekinetic girl wreaks havoc on her hometown of Chamberlain, Maine.

What is the meaning of "REDRUM" in Stephen King's *The Shining* (1977)?
The eerie word is "Murder" spelled backward.

Which films based on his stories has Stephen King directed?
Only one, *Maximum Overdrive* (1986). It is taken from his short story "Trucks," in the *Night Shift* collection (1978).

Who is the narrator of Umberto Eco's *The Name of the Rose* (1983)?
He is Adso de Melck, a young monk. Adso, the narrator, assists William of Baskerville, a Franciscan trying to solve a series of murders in a medieval monastery.

On what day does the nuclear war take place in *Warday* (1984)?
In Whitley Strieber and James Kunetka's novel, the brief nuclear war that devastates America takes place on October 28, 1988.

What is the logo for Macon Leary's travel book series in Anne Tyler's novel *The Accidental Tourist* (1985)?
A winged armchair adorns the covers of Leary's series of travel books for business travelers who want to pretend they never left home. Titles include *Accidental Tourist in France* and *Accidental Tourist in Germany*.

Who is murdered in *Presumed Innocent*?
In Scott Turow's 1987 novel, Carolyn Polhemus, an assistant district attorney, is murdered in her apart-

ment. The evidence points to fellow prosecutor—and jilted lover—Rusty Sabich.

What is the name of the investment banking firm for which Sherman McCoy works in Tom Wolfe's *The Bonfire of the Vanities* (1987)?
Pierce and Pierce, occupying the fiftieth to fifty-fourth floors of a Wall Street skyscraper.

What was serial killer Buffalo Bill's real name in Thomas Harris's *The Silence of the Lambs* (1988)?
Jame Gumb.

What are the names of the mothers and daughters in *The Joy Luck Club*?
The four sets of Chinese mothers and their American-born daughters who are the subjects of Amy Tan's 1989 novel are:

1. Suyuan Woo and her daughter Jing-mei "June" Woo
2. An-mei Hsu and her daughter Rose Hsu Jordan
3. Lindo Jong and her daughter Waverly Jong
4. Ying-ying St. Clair and her daughter Lena St. Clair

PUBLISHING

What is the oldest existing publisher?
It is Cambridge University Press, which was established in 1584.

When was the Gutenburg Bible published?
Circa 1456, at Mainz, Germany. It was the first printed Bible and the first large book set on movable metal type. German printer Johannes Gutenberg, inventor of movable type, is believed to have printed it, though Johann Fust and Peter Schöffer are also candidates.

What is a colophon?
The word can mean either a publisher's emblem or facts about a book's publication. These are now usually placed on the title page or near the beginning, but were formerly placed at the end.

What kind of book is a bibelot?
It is a miniature edition of great beauty, or more generally a literary trinket.

What is a chapbook?
A small, inexpensive book or pamphlet popular from the sixteenth to the eighteenth centuries. It was sold on the streets by "chapmen," or peddlers, and consisted usually of crime stories, biographies, ballads, or religious tracts.

What is the technical meaning of the printer's term "vignette"?
It is a small, unenclosed ornamental design on a blank space in a book, especially at the beginning or end of a chapter. By extension, a vignette is a short artistic work.

What is the difference between a folio and a quarto? An octavo and a duodecimo?
All of these terms refer to book sizes. In the first centuries of printing, book pages were of a standard size—13½ inches by 17 inches. These "foolscap" sheets, when folded one or more times, produced a "signature," a section that was bound with other signatures to produce the book. A folio was a signature

of two leaves, a quarto four leaves, an octavo eight leaves, and a duodecimo twelve leaves.

Who was the "Bowdler" behind the word "bowdlerize"?

Dr. Thomas Bowdler (1754–1825) published an expurgated volume of Shakespeare's works called *Family Shakespeare* in 1818. Bowdler removed obscene and salacious passages and replaced "God" with "Heaven" throughout.

How many copies of *Uncle Tom's Cabin* were sold when it was first published?

Within a year of its 1852 publication, the Harriet Beecher Stowe novel had sold 300,000 copies. The United States population at the time was 23 million, meaning that 1 of every 77 citizens owned a copy.

Who was the first literary agent?

Alexander Pollock Watt (1834–1914) of England is often considered the founder of the business. His clients included Thomas Hardy and Rudyard Kipling.

What was the price of the first Everyman's Library volumes?

One shilling per copy. They were first published in London by Joseph Malaby Dent in 1905. The imprint was revived by Knopf in 1991.

How many publishers rejected James Joyce's *Dubliners*?

Joyce's collection of short stories was rejected by at least twenty-two publishers. Grant Richards finally printed the collection in 1914.

When was Alfred Knopf, Publishers, founded?
In 1915, by Alfred and Blanche Knopf.

When did Alfred Knopf, Publishers, and Random House merge?
Knopf became part of Random House in April 1960.

Who started Vintage Books (the paperback imprint of Knopf)?
Alfred Knopf, Jr., son of Alfred Knopf.

Where and when did the first "Shakespeare and Company" bookstore open?
The English-language bookshop and lending library was opened by Sylvia Beach in Paris on November 17, 1919.

How old was F. Scott Fitzgerald when his first novel was published?
He was twenty-three when *This Side of Paradise* appeared in 1920—making him the youngest novelist ever published by Scribners.

What was the original royalty paid on a paperback book?
Pocket Books, the first paperback publisher, paid authors one cent per copy sold up to the first 50,000 copies and one and a half cents for each additional copy. For a twenty-five cent book, this meant 4 percent and 6 percent, respectively.

What publishing company did T. S. Eliot work for?
Faber and Faber, beginning in 1925.

When did Ernest Hemingway meet his future editor Maxwell Perkins?
On February 9, 1926, after several letters from Perkins trying to get Hemingway to switch publishers from Boni & Liveright to Scribners. On their first meeting in New York, the author and editor struck a deal on *The Torrents of Spring* and *The Sun Also Rises*. Perkins's first impression of Hemingway: "He is a most interesting chap about his bullfighting and boxing."

What was the last book edited by Maxwell Perkins?
James Jones's *From Here to Eternity* (1951). The Scribners editor had also worked on Alan Paton's *Cry the Beloved Country* (1948) and Marcia Davenport's *East Side, West Side* (1947) in the months before his death on June 17, 1947.

What was the first book published by Random House?
Voltaire's *Candide* in 1928, a new edition designed and illustrated by Rockwell Kent. The founders of Random House were Bennett Cerf and Donald Klopfer.

Who was the original owner of the Modern Library?
Horace Liveright, founder of Liveright and Sons. It was purchased from him by Bennett Cerf and Donald Klopfer.

When were the first Penguin books published?
In 1935 by British publisher Allen Lane. The first ten Penguin paperbacks included Agatha Christie's *The*

Mysterious Affair at Styles, Ernest Hemingway's *A Farewell to Arms,* André Maurois's *Ariel,* and Dorothy L. Sayers's *The Unpleasantness at the Bellona Club.*

What was the first paperback to be published with several different covers in the first printing?
Future Shock (1971) by Alvin Toffler. Covers in different neon colors were issued.

Which sells more, fiction or nonfiction books?
Nonfiction, by four to one.

THE QUESTION AND ANSWER HALL OF FAME

In what book of Plato's *Republic* (c. fourth century
B.C.) does the Cave Allegory appear?
Book VII.

According to Dante's *Inferno* (1321), who is at the
bottom of Hell?
In the lowest circle of hell, the place for traitors, a
three-faced Satan chews on three people: Brutus and
Cassius, betrayers of Julius Caesar, and Judas Iscar-
iot, betrayer of Jesus.

How many husbands did Chaucer's Wife of Bath
have?
Five.

What is the complete text of Hamlet's "To be, or not to be" soliloquy?
As it appears in *Hamlet* (c. 1601), act 3, scene 1, lines 55-87, the speech goes as follows:
    To be, or not to be: that is the question.
Whether 'tis nobler in the mind to suffer
The slings and arrows of outrageous fortune,
Or to take arms against a sea of troubles,
And by opposing end them. To die; to sleep;
No more; and by a sleep to say we end
The heart-ache and the thousand natural shocks
That flesh is heir to. 'Tis a consummation
Devoutly to be wish'd. To die, to sleep;—
To sleep? Perchance to dream! Ay, there's the
    rub;
For in that sleep of death what dreams may
    come,
When we have shuffled off this mortal coil,
Must give us pause. There's the respect
That makes calamity of so long life.
For who would bear the whips and scorns of
    time,
The oppressor's wrong, the proud man's con-
    tumely,
The pangs of dispriz'd love, the law's delay,
The insolence of office, and the spurns
That patient merit of the unworthy takes,
When he himself might his quietus make
With a bare bodkin? who would fardels bear,
To grunt and sweat under a weary life,
But that the dread of something after death,
The undiscover'd country from whose bourn
No traveller returns, puzzles the will

And makes us rather bear those ills we have
Than fly to others that we know not of?
Thus conscience does make cowards of us all;
And thus the native hue of resolution
Is sicklied o'er with the pale cast of thought,
And enterprises of great pith and moment
With this regard their currents turn awry,
And lose the name of action.

What is the longest novel in the English language?
Samuel Richardson's *Clarissa* (1747–48), at about one million words.

What was Goethe's first name?
His name was Johann Wolfgang von Goethe (1749–1832).

What did Coleridge consider "the three most perfect plots ever planned"?
Sophocles' *Oedipus Rex* (c. 426 B.C.), Ben Jonson's *The Alchemist* (1610), and Henry Fielding's *Tom Jones* (1749).

Who is the title character in James Fenimore Cooper's *The Last of the Mohicans* (1826)?
Uncas, son of Chingachgook. He is killed defending Cora, his love, against Magua.

What are the names of the Three Musketeers?
Alexandre Dumas's trio in *The Three Musketeers* (1844) are Athos, Porthos, and Aramis. D'Artagnan is not one of the titular characters.

Which Brontë sister wrote *Jane Eyre* (1847) and which wrote *Wuthering Heights* (1847)?
Charlotte wrote *Jane Eyre* and Emily wrote *Wuthering Heights*. As a mnemonic, try remembering that "Emily" and "Wuthering" each have three syllables.

How many ways does Elizabeth Barrett Browning love her beloved in "How Do I Love Thee?" (1850)?
She counts eight:
1. To the depth and breadth and height my soul can reach
2. To the level of every day's most quiet need
3. Freely, as men strive for Right
4. Purely, as they turn from Praise
5. With the passion put to use in my old griefs
6. With my childhood's faith
7. With a love I seemed to lose with my lost saints
8. With the breath, smiles, tears of all my life
"If God choose," she adds, "I shall but love thee better after death."

What is the origin of the phrase, "Happy families are all alike, every unhappy family is unhappy in its own way"?
Leo Tolstoy's novel *Anna Karenina* (1873–76) begins with this often quoted insight.

What gifts are traded in O. Henry's short story "The Gift of the Magi" (1905)?
In the story, a young husband, Jim Young, sells his prized watch to buy a set of combs for his wife Della's

hair. Della has her hair cut and sold to buy Jim a watch fob. The story first appeared in the New York *Sunday World Magazine* in 1902.

Who dies in *Death in Venice*?
In Thomas Mann's 1912 novella, Gustave von Aschenbach, a middle-aged German writer, becomes consumed with a passion for a young Polish boy, which leads to von Aschenbach's death.

In Fitzgerald's *The Great Gatsby* (1925), what is Jay Gatsby's real name?
James Gatz.

What does the "T.S." in T. S. Eliot stand for?
Thomas Stearns.

What does the "e.e." in e.e. cummings stand for?
Edward Estlin.

What is the first line of Margaret Mitchell's *Gone With the Wind* (1936)?
"Scarlett O'Hara was not beautiful, but men seldom realized it when caught by her charm as the Tarleton twins were."

> **What is the last?**
> "After all, tomorrow is another day."

Is there an apostrophe in the title of James Joyce's *Finnegans Wake* (1939)?
No.

In Arthur Miller's *Death of a Salesman* (1949), what does Willy Loman sell?
He is a traveling salesman of ladies' lingerie.

Where and when did Ernest Hemingway shoot himself?
Ketchum, Idaho, on July 2, 1961.

To what poem is Joan Didion referring in the title of her book *Slouching Toward Bethlehem* (1968)?
She refers to the last line of "The Second Coming" (1921) by William Butler Yeats: "And what rough beast, its hour come round at last,/Slouches toward Bethlehem to be born?"

SCRAPES
WITH THE LAW

Why was Boethius imprisoned?
Ancius Manlius Severinus Boethius was imprisoned for treason by Theodoric the Great, the Ostrogoth ruler of Rome. While in prison, he wrote the work for which he is famous, *The Consolation of Philosophy*. He was executed in 525 A.D.

Why was Cervantes imprisoned?
He was imprisoned on a charge of fraud while working as a government tax inspector. During his prison term he began writing *Don Quixote* (1605). It was his

second period of captivity: he had also been captured once by Algerian pirates.

When and for what was Milton imprisoned?
He was arrested in 1660 after he published *The Ready and Easy Way to Establish a Free Commonwealth*, advocating republican government, just as King Charles II was restored to power. Fellow writers Sir William D'Avenant and Andrew Marvell interceded on his behalf, and he was released.

Did the Marquis de Sade (1740–1814) ever spend time in prison?
Yes, the author of *La Philosophie dans le Boudoir* (1795) spent twenty-seven years, off and on, in prison, convicted for sex offenses and for writing obscene books.

What Oliver Goldsmith work was sold to prevent his arrest for debt?
The novel *The Vicar of Wakefield* (1766). His friend Samuel Johnson sold it on his behalf for sixty pounds.

Why did Charles Lamb (1775–1834) have to take care of his sister?
The English essayist took care of his insane sister, Mary Lamb, after she killed their mother in 1796. Mary died in 1847.

What night did Henry David Thoreau spend in the Concord, Massachusetts, town jail?
July 23, 1846, after refusing to pay his poll tax in

protest of the Mexican War. The story is told in Thoreau's essay "Civil Disobedience" (1848).

Why was Dostoevsky imprisoned?
He was sentenced to four years in the labor camp at Omsk, Siberia, for political crimes. Among other things, he and his Petrashevsky circle were charged with reading a banned letter and conspiring to set up an unauthorized printing press. They were arrested in 1849.

What was the French court decision on Baudelaire's book *Les Fleurs du Mal*?
The 1864 book of poetry caused the French court to arrest the author and fine him 300 francs.

What fellow poet wounded Arthur Rimbaud with a pistol?
Paul Verlaine, in 1873. Verlaine shot him in the wrist during an argument and was punished by imprisonment.

For what crime was O. Henry imprisoned?
William Sidney Porter (O. Henry) (1862–1910) was convicted of embezzlement while working as a bank teller. He was sentenced to three years in jail. It was during this time that he started to write stories.

Of what crime was Émile Zola convicted?
In 1898–99, he was convicted of libel in France for his letter "J'Accuse." The open letter to the French president defended Captain Alfred Dreyfus, a Jewish of-

ficer accused of treason. After the conviction, Zola fled to exile in England for a year, before returning to France as a hero.

Of what crime was Oscar Wilde (1854–1900) convicted? How long was his sentence?

He was convicted of homosexuality and sentenced to two years' imprisonment with hard labor. He served his sentence from 1895 to 1897.

When was *Ulysses* allowed to be published in the United States?

It was permitted to be transported to the United States for publication in 1933, following a ruling in the U.S. District Court of New York by Judge John M. Woolsey, in which the book was deemed to be "somewhat emetic" but not "an aphrodisiac."

When was Dalton Trumbo summoned before the House Committee on Un-American Activities?

In 1947. The screenwriter and author of *Johnny Got His Gun* (1939) was imprisoned and blacklisted for his refusal to answer questions about his Communist affiliations.

Who was arrested for selling Allen Ginsberg's poem "Howl" (1956)?

Beat poet and publisher Lawrence Ferlinghetti was arrested in his San Francisco store, City Lights Bookshop, in May 1957. The book was said to have no "redeeming social importance."

SCRAPES WITH THE LAW

For what crimes did Eldridge Cleaver spend time in prison?
In 1954, he began a sentence at Soledad State Prison for possession of marijuana. Later he served time at Folsom Prison for, in his words, a "rape-on-principle." While in prison, he began *Soul on Ice* (1968).

When was Aleksandr Solzhenitsyn expelled from the Soviet Union?
February 13, 1974.

When did the Iranian government condemn writer Salman Rushdie to death?
Ayatollah Khomeini issued a death sentence against the author of *The Satanic Verses* on February 15, 1989. Rushdie has been in hiding since.

SHAKESPEARE

What is the shortest play by William Shakespeare?
Macbeth (c. 1606), at 2108 lines.

   What is the longest?
   Hamlet (c. 1601), at 3931 lines.

How many children did Shakespeare have?
Three: Susanna (baptized 1583) and twins, Hamnet
and Judith (baptized 1585).

**How many Shakespeare sonnets are addressed to a
woman?**
The last 26 of the 154 sonnets are addressed to a

woman, known as the "Dark Lady." The first 126 are addressed to a young man.

In what Shakespeare plays do these members of royalty appear?
1. The Countess of Rousillon—*All's Well That Ends Well* (1602)
2. Duke Frederick—*As You Like It* (1599–1600)
3. Fortinbras, Prince of Norway—*Hamlet* (1600–1601)
4. Macduff, the Thane of Fife—*Macbeth* (1606)
5. Claudio, Lord of Florence—*Much Ado About Nothing* (1598–99)

Who wrote the disparaging reference to Shakespeare as "an upstart crow, beautified with our feathers . . . [who] being an absolute *Johannes fac totum,* is in his own conceit the only Shake-scene in a country"?
Playwright Robert Greene in the pamphlet "A Groatsworth of Wit Bought with a Million of Repentance" (1592).

What Shakespeare character says "The first thing we do, let's kill all the lawyers"?
Dick the butcher says it in *Henry the Sixth, Part 2* (c. 1590), act 4, scene 2, line 84. His proposal is made in support of Jack Cade's plans for a revolution in England.

Who are the title characters in *The Two Gentlemen of Verona* (c. 1592)?
Valentine and Proteus.

What rank did the title character of *Richard III* (c. 1594) hold before he became king?
He was the Duke of Gloucester.

What is the name of the play within the play in *A Midsummer Night's Dream* (c. 1594)?
Pyramus and Thisbe, a "tragical comedy."

What Shakespearean lover says, "The course of true love never did run smooth"?
Lysander says this to his star-crossed lover Hermia in *A Midsummer Night's Dream* (c. 1594), act 1, scene 1, line 134.

In *Romeo and Juliet* (c. 1595), which is the Montague and which the Capulet?
Romeo is a Montague and Juliet a Capulet. One way of remembering is that "Juliet" and "Capulet" both end in "et."

What does the "wherefore" mean in "O Romeo, Romeo! wherefore art thou Romeo?"
It means "for what purpose"—not "where." In this line from *Romeo and Juliet* (c. 1595), act 2, scene 2, line 33, Juliet, on her balcony, rhetorically asks the absent Romeo why he should have that name. His identity is a source of strife, since his family and hers are feuding.

Who is the merchant in *The Merchant of Venice* (c. 1596)?
Not Shylock. The merchant is Antonio, who borrows

money from Shylock to help out his friend Bassanio. Antonio agrees to surrender a pound of flesh if he defaults on the loan.

What Shakespearean king says, "Uneasy lies the head that wears a crown"?
King Henry IV of England in *Henry the Fourth, Part 2* (c. 1598), act 3, scene 1, line 31.

Who is the jester in *As You Like It* (c. 1599)?
Touchstone.

> **In *King Lear* (c. 1605)?**
> He is simply called "Fool."

What Shakespeare character says, "All the world's a stage,/And all the men and women merely players"?
Jaques in *As You Like It* (c. 1599), act 2, scene 7, lines 139–43.

What breach is Henry V talking about when he exhorts his men to go "Once more into the breach"?
In *Henry V* (c. 1599), act 3, scene 1, the English king urges his men to rush at the breach in the wall of the French port town of Harfleur.

What Shakespeare sonnet begins, "Shall I compare thee to a summer's day?"
Sonnet 18.

What exactly is the line about "method to my madness" in Shakespeare?
"Though this be madness, yet there is method in't."

Polonius says it about Hamlet's feigned madness in *Hamlet* (c. 1601), act 2, scene 2, lines 208–9.

What is the exact wording of the line about rottenness in Denmark?
"Something is rotten in the state of Denmark." Marcellus says it to Horatio in *Hamlet*, act 1, scene 4, line 90.

What were Shakespeare's sources for *Hamlet* (c. 1601)?
The earliest source is *Historica Danica* (1514) by the Danish historian Saxo Grammaticus. That chronicle was translated by Pierre de Belleforest in *Histoires Tragiques* (1570). Shakespeare also drew on a play, now lost, that appeared around 1589. That play is commonly known as "source Hamlet" or "Ur-Hamlet."

What actor first played Hamlet?
Richard Burbage (c. 1567–1619). Burbage also was the first to play Shakespeare's King Lear, Othello, and Richard III.

What is the longest role in Shakespeare?
The title character in *Hamlet* (c. 1601), has 1,422 lines, nearly 250 more than Falstaff speaks in *Henry IV* Parts I and II (c. 1597–98) combined.

What is a Moor?
The Moors were the mixed Arab and Berber conquerors of Spain in the eighth century. In literature, the

most famous member of this ethnic group is Othello, the Moor of Venice (c. 1604).

What are the names of Lear's daughters in *King Lear* (c. 1605)?
Goneril is the eldest; Regan is the middle child; Cordelia is the youngest.

What title does Macbeth hold at the beginning of Shakespeare's *Macbeth* (1606)? What title does he gain?
The play begins with Macbeth as the thane of Glamis. He becomes thane of Cawdor and eventually king of Scotland.

From where in Shakespeare's plays did Aldous Huxley get the title of his *Brave New World* (1932)?
The Tempest (c. 1611), act 5, scene 1, lines 183–84. Miranda, Prospero's daughter, says "O brave new world/That has such people in't!"

Who was Shakespeare's collaborator on *Henry the Eighth* (c. 1612–13)?
Younger playwright John Fletcher. Shakespeare also wrote some parts of Fletcher's *The Two Noble Kinsmen* (1613).

What play was being performed when the Globe Theatre caught fire and burned?
Shakespeare's *Henry the Eighth*, on June 29, 1613.

When did the First Folio edition of Shakespeare's works appear?

This first printed collection of Shakespeare's plays was published in 1623, seven years after the author's death. It included all of the plays except *Pericles* (c. 1608).

Who popularized the theory that Francis Bacon wrote Shakespeare's plays?

It was Delia Bacon (1811–59), who was no relation to the author she studied. In her book *Plays of Shakespeare Unfolded* (1857), she said that Francis Bacon and his friends actually wrote the plays now attributed to Shakespeare. The book was received unfavorably, and its author soon went insane and died, but the theory has resurfaced from time to time.

What is "honorificabilitudinitatibus"?

It means "with honorableness," and appears in Shakespeare's *Love's Labour's Lost* (c. 1594), act 5, scene 1. Some scholars have noted pointedly that the word can be rearranged into the Latin sentence "*Hi ludi F. Bacon's nati tuiti orbi,*" meaning: "These plays, F. Bacon's offspring, are preserved for the world."

How many books and papers are published about Shakespeare each year?

The average is over 3,000 per year.

What was the name of the "new" poem attributed to Shakespeare in the 1980s?

It was a ninety-line poem called "Shall I Die?" unearthed by scholar Gary Taylor in November 1985. The poem appears as Shakespeare's in a manuscript anthology of poems dated 1630, but the attribution was long ignored, since such anthologies are usually considered unreliable. Taylor argued that the poem is Shakespeare's, written about the time of *Romeo and Juliet* (1594–95). Most other scholars have disagreed, saying the poetry is much too weak.

What does Shakespeare's gravestone read?
His epitaph is "Blessed be the man that spares these stones/And cursed be he that moves my bones."

TABLE TALK

Who said, "No man but a blockhead ever wrote, except for money"?
Samuel Johnson (1709–84).

To what work was Samuel Johnson referring when he said: "I am shocked to hear you quote from so vicious a book. I am sorry to hear you have read it; a confession which no modest lady should ever make. I scarcely know a more corrupt work"?
Henry Fielding's *Tom Jones* (1749).

Who was described, "Three-fifths of him genius and two-fifths of him fudge"?
It was Edgar Allan Poe, according to the contempo-

rary American poet and critic James Russell Lowell (1819–91). The quote appears in Lowell's poem "A Fable for Critics."

Upon the publication of *Leaves of Grass,* who wrote to Walt Whitman, "I greet you at the beginning of a great career"?
Ralph Waldo Emerson in 1850. The complete salutation is: "I greet you at the beginning of a great career, which yet must have had a long foregound somewhere for such a start." Whitman was thirty-six at the time of the book's publication.

Who said of Shakespeare's *King Lear* (c. 1605), "A strange, horrible business, but I suppose good enough for Shakespeare's day"?
Queen Victoria.

Who said, "If I confine myself to boy life at times, it is because that life had a peculiar charm for me, and not because I was unfamiliar with other phases of life"?
Samuel Langhorne Clemens, or Mark Twain.

Who was called "the Lincoln of Literature"?
Mark Twain was so named by critic and author William Dean Howells (1837–1920).

Who called George Eliot's *Middlemarch* (1871–72) "the magnificent book which with all its imperfections is one of the few English novels for grown up people"?
Virginia Woolf.

Who said, "My idea of paradise is a perfect automobile going thirty miles an hour on a smooth road to a twelfth-century cathedral"?
Henry Adams (1838–1918), grandson of John Quincy Adams, great-grandson of John Adams, and author of *The Education of Henry Adams* (1907).

Who said, "There's no money in poetry, but then there's no poetry in money either"?
Robert Graves.

What did H. L. Mencken think were the three traps for a writer?
Alcohol, women, and politics.

Who listed his writing requirements as "paper, tobacco, food, and a little whiskey"?
William Faulkner.

Who told Hemingway he was "ninety percent Rotarian"?
Gertrude Stein (1874–1946).

Whom did Clifton Fadiman call "a past master in making nothing happen very slowly"?
Gertrude Stein.

Who said, "The demand that I make of my reader is that he should devote his whole life to reading my books"?
James Joyce (1882–1941).

Who said, "Every author is a son-of-a-bitch"?
Theodore Dreiser, to Bennett Cerf.

Of whom did Edmund Wilson write, "His style has the desperate jauntiness of an orchestra fiddling away for dear life on a sinking ship"?
Evelyn Waugh (1903–66).

Who, when asked by an editor to cut her novel, said, "Would you cut the Bible"?
Ayn Rand, about *Atlas Shrugged* (1957).

Who said, "There's nothing to writing. All you do is sit down at a typewriter and open a vein"?
Sportswriter Red (Walter Wellesley) Smith.

WRITERS'
LIVES

Was Dante (1265–1321) a Guelph or a Ghibelline?
He was a Bianchi, originally a faction within the
Guelph party but later allied with the Ghibellines. In
the long struggle between the papacy and the Holy
Roman Empire, the Guelphs supported the Papacy
and the Ghibellines supported the Emperor.

What was Chaucer's last job?
Chaucer (1343–1400) was deputy forester in the
King's Forest at Petherton in Somerset during the
1390s. The son of a vintner, he had held many government jobs throughout his life, including controller
of customs in London and justice of the peace in Kent.

In what battle was Cervantes wounded?
He was wounded in the naval Battle of Lepanto
(1571). He was wounded twice in the chest and once
in the left hand; he lost the use of the latter for life.

**How much money did Shakespeare make for writing
a play?**
A typical play, *Hamlet*, earned him five pounds, exactly what Milton earned for writing *Paradise Lost*.

**How was poet Andrew Marvell employed by John
Milton?**
He was Milton's assistant in the late 1650s, when Milton was Latin secretary for Oliver Cromwell's government.

When did Milton go blind?
He became aware of his growing blindness in the
1640s, when he was in his thirties. By 1651, when he
was forty-three, he was completely blind. *Paradise
Lost* was completed several years later and published
in 1667.

**When was Jonathan Swift (1667–1745) ordained a
priest?**
Swift became an Anglican priest on January 13, 1695.
He was assigned to Kilroot, Ireland.

When did Daniel Defoe change his name?
Daniel Foe changed his last name to the more socially
upward-sounding Defoe in 1703. The name was an
aid to his writing career.

What position in English government did Joseph Addison (1672–1719) hold?

The publisher of the *Tatler* and the *Spectator* served as a member of Parliament from 1708 until his death.

How tall was Alexander Pope?

The eighteenth-century English poet was four feet, six inches tall. His growth was stunted by a childhood illness (probably Pott's disease), a tubercular infection of the spine.

When did Dr. Johnson (1709–84) receive his doctorate?

In 1755, just before publication of *A Dictionary of the English Language.* The Oxford degree was awarded despite the fact that Johnson had failed to graduate from Pembroke College, Oxford, back in 1729.

When did James Boswell and Samuel Johnson meet?

On May 16, 1763, in the back parlor of Thomas Davies's bookshop in London. Boswell (1749–95) was in his mid-twenties, Johnson his mid-fifties. The two remained friends until Johnson's death. Boswell's *The Life of Samuel Johnson* appeared in 1791.

When was Edward Gibbon a member of the English Parliament?

He served in Parliament from 1774 to 1783, during which time he was also writing and publishing *The Decline and Fall of the Roman Empire* (1776–88, six volumes).

What birth defect did Lord Byron (1788–1824) have?
A clubfoot.

When did Byron join the Greek fight for independence from the Turkish Empire?
In 1824. He trained troops briefly at Missolonghi but died of malarial fever the same year. His heart and lungs were buried in Greece; the rest of him went back to the family vault in England.

What was the name of the brother of the Brontë sisters?
Branwell, a failed artist dependent upon opium, alcohol, and his successful sisters.

Did Thoreau go to college?
Yes, he graduated from Harvard but would not accept his degree. He said it was not "worth five dollars."

Who was called the "Sage of Chelsea"?
Thomas Carlyle (1795–1881), author of *Sartor Resartus* (1833–34), and resident of Chelsea, England.

Who was the "Sage of Concord"?
Ralph Waldo Emerson (1803–82) of Concord, Massachusetts.

When did Frederick Douglass escape from slavery?
The Maryland-born slave (c. 1817–95) escaped in 1838 and traveled to Massachusetts. He published his *Narrative of the Life of Frederick Douglass* in 1845.

When did Herman Melville serve on a whaling ship?
For eighteen months from January 1841 to July 1842, Melville (1819–91) served on the whaler *Acushnet*. He deserted the ship at the Marquesas Islands with a companion, Richard Tobias Greene. After further adventures on the islands and at sea, Melville returned to America in 1844. His whaling experiences became one of the sources for *Moby-Dick* (1851).

What was Nathaniel Hawthorne's job in customs?
He was a surveyor at the Boston Custom House from 1839 to 1841, and also at the Salem Custom House from 1846 to 1849.

How long was Melville a customs inspector?
Melville served at this post in New York City for nineteen years beginning in 1863. He died virtually forgotten in 1891. His work was not "rediscovered" by critics until 1920.

When did Dickens first visit the United States?
He made his first visit in 1842, when he met with Washington Irving, whom he admired, and whose work he said he took to bed with him "two nights out of seven."

When did Oscar Wilde begin his lecture tour of the United States?
He set off for America on Christmas Eve 1881. Upon reaching the United States, he was asked if he had anything to declare to customs, and said, "Only my genius."

When was Walt Whitman the editor of the *Brooklyn Daily Eagle*?
In 1846–47.

When did Emily Dickinson start dressing only in white?
She began to do so after 1862; after 1865 she spent most of her time in her upstairs room. It is possible she did both in response to her fear of other people or of death.

When did Sir Richard Francis Burton make his pilgrimage to Mecca?
Disguised as a Muslim from India, the English diplomat and adventurer visited the sacred Arabian city in 1853. He also discovered Lake Tanganyika, with John Hanning Speke, in 1858. He is best known to literature for his translation of *The Arabian Nights* in 1885–88.

When did Mark Twain (1835–1910) work on a steamboat on the Mississippi?
From 1857 to 1861—two years as an apprentice and two years as a licensed pilot.

Where was Joseph Conrad (1857–1924) born?
One of the masters of English literature, Conrad was born in the Polish Ukraine in 1857. He never became a fluent speaker of English.

How long was he a sailor?
For twenty years, from 1874 to 1894. After quitting the sea and settling in England, Conrad pub-

lished his first novel at the age of thirty-eight: *Almayer's Folly* (1895).

When did Christian essayist John Henry Newman (1801–90) convert to Roman Catholicism?
In 1845.

> **When was he ordained a priest?**
> In 1846.

> **When was he made a cardinal?**
> In 1879.

What was Lewis Carroll's occupation?
Charles Dodgson, author (as Lewis Carroll) of *Alice's Adventures in Wonderland* (1865), was an Oxford professor of mathematics and logic.

What did Thomas Hardy (1840–1928) do before he became a full-time writer?
He was an architect. The success of his fourth published novel, *Far from the Madding Crowd* (1874), allowed him to leave his job, get married, and devote himself to writing.

What two colleges did Robert Frost enter and then leave?
He entered Dartmouth in 1892, and left shortly thereafter. He entered Harvard in 1897, and remained for two years, but did not complete a degree.

Who was Max Brod?
Brod was a friend of Franz Kafka's who promised the

dying writer that he would destroy all of Kafka's manuscripts. He did not keep his promise.

Was William Sydney Porter (O. Henry) any relation to Katherine Anne Porter?
They were cousins.

When did Henry James become a British subject?
The New York-born novelist (1843–1916) became a British subject in July 1915, shortly before his death, after living in Britain for nearly forty years.

How long did Raymond Chandler live in England?
The writer of quintessentially American detective fiction lived in England from age seven until age twenty-four. He returned to the United States in 1912.

When and where during World War I was Ernest Hemingway wounded?
A Red Cross volunteer, Hemingway was wounded near Fossalta, Italy, on July 8, 1918.

When did Marcel Proust dip his madeleine in a cup of tea, inspiring his *Remembrance of Things Past* (1913–27)?
January 1909.

From where did Flannery O'Connor get the peacocks she raised on her farm?
She ordered them from a 1952 ad in the Florida *Market Bulletin* offering three-year-old peafowl at sixty-five dollars a pair. They were sent by Railway Express,

from Eustis, Florida: a peacock, a hen, and four seven-week old peabiddies.

What was Sinclair Lewis's nickname?
Red.

What was Robert Penn Warren's nickname?
Red.

When did E. M. Forster travel to India?
The author of *A Passage to India* made his own passage there in 1921, to become secretary to the Maharaja of Dewas Senior.

Where did poet William Carlos Williams go to medical school?
At the University of Pennsylvania.

Did T. S. Eliot (1888–1965) have a Ph.D.?
No. He received an A.B. and A.M. at Harvard and studied at the Sorbonne and at Oxford.

What was J. R. R. Tolkien's area of specialty as a scholar?
The author of *The Hobbit* (1937) and *The Lord of the Rings* (1954–56) was a philologist and professor of medieval literature at Oxford University.

When was Yeats a senator?
William Butler Yeats (1865–1939) served in the senate of the Irish Free State from 1922 to 1928. He generally supported Protestant landed interests.

What did Upton Sinclair's campaign slogan—EPIC—stand for?
"End Poverty in California." It was the umbrella term for his democratic platform for his 1934 campaign for governor. This platform contained such programs as a graduated income tax and retirement pensions. Sinclair won the Democratic nomination, but after a bitter campaign lost to Republican candidate Frank Merriam.

When did Norman Mailer run for mayor of New York City?
In 1969. His campaign slogan was "No More Bullshit." One of his platform positions was that New York State secede from the union and become a separate state. He finished fourth in a race of five candidates.

When did J. D. Salinger meet Ernest Hemingway?
They met after the initial assault on the beaches of Normandy on D-Day, June 6, 1944. Both had been in Europe during World War II: Salinger was in the Army and was part of the attack on Utah Beach; Hemingway was a war correspondent. After this meeting, Salinger sent letters to Hemingway.

When did Vladimir Nabokov (1899–1977) become interested in butterflies?
According to his autobiography, *Speak, Memory* (1966), it started when he was seven years old. He writes: "From the age of seven, everything I felt in connection with a rectangle of framed sunlight was

dominated by a single passion. If my first glance of the morning was for the sun, my first thought was for the butterflies it would engender."

What writer lived next door to Truman Capote as a child?
Harper Lee, author of *To Kill a Mockingbird* (1960). Lee modeled the character Dill after the young Capote.

What is V. S. Naipaul's nationality?
The essayist and novelist was born in Trinidad in 1932 of Indian parents. He has lived in England since 1950.

What does the "V.S." stand for?
Vidiadhar Surajprasad.

What is John le Carré's real name?
David John Moore Cornwell.

Was columnist and spy novelist William F. Buckley ever in the CIA?
After graduating from Yale, Buckley joined the Central Intelligence Agency and worked under E. Howard Hunt in Mexico in 1951 and 1952. Buckley is the godfather of three of Hunt's children; he refuses to discuss his work in the CIA.

Did Ken Kesey have any firsthand experience with psychiatric wards?
In 1961, the author of the novel *One Flew Over the Cuckoo's Nest* (1962) worked as a night attendant in

the psychiatric ward at the Veteran's Administration Hospital in Menlo Park, California.

When did LeRoi Jones become Amiri Baraka?
The New Jersey–born poet and playwright (1934–) changed his name to Imamu Amiri Baraka in 1965, upon converting to Islam. His works include the play *Dutchman* (1964) and *Daggers and Javelins: Essays* (1984).

Where did mystery writer John D. MacDonald get his M.B.A.?
Harvard Business School.

What subject area did novelist Anne Tyler study in her graduate work at Columbia University?
Russian studies. She once worked as Russian bibliographer at Duke University Library.

Who is the psychiatrist who released tapes of poet Anne Sexton's private sessions for Diane Wood Middlebrook's *Anne Sexton: A Biography* (1991)?
Dr. Martin T. Orne sparked controversy by releasing the tapes to the biographer. Sexton's daughter and literary executor, Linda Gray Sexton, agreed to have the tapes revealed.

How can you reach Thomas Pynchon?
His exact whereabouts are not publicly known, but he can be reached c/o Little, Brown and Company, 34 Beacon Street, Boston, MA 02106.

How can you reach J. D. Salinger?
You can try contacting his agent: Harold Ober Associates, 40 East 49th Street, New York, New York 10017. Salinger lives in seclusion in New Hampshire.

TRICK
QUESTIONS
AND POPULAR
DELUSIONS

Where in Shakespeare does the line "Methinks the lady doth protest too much" appear?
Nowhere. However, in *Hamlet* (c. 1601), act 3, scene 2, lines 222–230, Queen Gertrude says to Hamlet (while commenting on a character in a play), "The lady doth protest too much, methinks." The word "protest" here means "vow" or "affirm," not "object" or "decry."

Who wrote "Music has charms to soothe the savage beast"?
Not William Congreve, who wrote "Music has

charms to soothe a savage breast" in his play *The Mourning Bride* (1697), act 1, scene 1.

Who wrote "Hell hath no fury like a woman scorned"?

It is also attributed to William Congreve, but his exact words are, "Heaven has no rage like love to hatred turned,/Nor hell a fury like a woman scorned," in *The Mourning Bride*, act 3, scene 8.

What was Stendhal's first name?

The name stands alone. "Stendhal" was the pen name of novelist and critic Marie-Henri Beyle (1783–1842).

Who wrote "The Night Before Christmas"?

No one. The actual title of this poem is "A Visit from St. Nicholas," written by Clement Clark Moore for his nine children in 1822, and published anonymously in the *Troy Sentinel* in 1823.

What is the first line of *Moby-Dick* (1851)?

It is not the oft-quoted "Call me Ishmael," but rather, "The pale Usher—threadbare in coat, heart, body and brain; I see him now." This sentence opens the first of two background sections on the whale, "Etymology." It is followed by "Extracts," a collection of quotes on the whale, and then the first chapter, "Loomings," which begins, "Call me Ishmael."

In which Sir Arthur Conan Doyle story does Sherlock Holmes first speak the memorable "Elementary, my dear Watson"?
Holmes never utters the phrase in a Doyle story. The closest he comes is to say "Elementary" in "The Crooked Man" (1894).

What color are Dorothy's slippers in L. Frank Baum's *The Wonderful Wizard of Oz* (1900)?
Silver. The 1939 movie made them ruby.

In "Anecdote of the Jar" (1923), what does Wallace Stevens (1879–1955) say is in the jar that is placed on a hill in Tennessee?
He describes the jar as "gray and bare," but does not specifically say what it contains.

What was the hair color of Anita Loos, author of *Gentlemen Prefer Blondes* (1925)?
Brown.

Who is the subject of *The Autobiography of Alice B. Toklas* (1933)?
Gertrude Stein. It is a memoir of Stein's life, written by Stein, but from the viewpoint of Alice B. Toklas. Toklas wrote her own autobiography in 1963, *What I Remembered*.

What is the longest novel ever written?
It is not Proust's *Remembrance of Things Past*. It is *Les Hommes de Bonne Volonté* by Jules Romains. The work, which was written between 1932 and 1947,

runs twenty-seven volumes. The English version runs fourteen volumes.

Where in Tennessee did Tennessee Williams come from?
He didn't come from Tennessee. Thomas Lanier Williams (1911–83) was born in Mississippi.

BIBLIOGRAPHY

Numerous primary sources—novels, plays, poems, and essays—were consulted for this book. Below are some of the secondary sources and collections that were also consulted.

Abrams, M. H., gen. ed. *The Norton Anthology of English Literature, rev. ed.* New York, NY: W. W. Norton & Co., 1968.

Bate, Walter Jackson, ed. *Criticism: The Major Texts, rev. ed.* New York, NY: Harcourt Brace Jovanovich, 1970.

Benét's Reader's Encyclopedia. New York, NY: Harper & Row, 1987.

Berg, A. Scott. *Maxwell Perkins: Editor of Genius.* New York, NY: Pocket Books, 1978.

Bevington, David. *Medieval Drama.* Boston, MA: Houghton Mifflin, 1975.

BIBLIOGRAPHY

Blair, Walter, et al. *The Literature of the United States, 3rd ed.* Glenview, IL: Scott, Foresman and Co., 1970.

Block, Haskell M., and Robert Shedd, ed. *Masters of Modern Drama.* New York, NY: McGraw-Hill, 1962.

Boyce, Charles. *Shakespeare A-Z.* New York, NY: Facts On File, 1990.

Carpenter, Humphrey, and Mari Prichard. *The Oxford Companion to Children's Literature.* New York, NY: Oxford University Press, 1984.

Cassill, R. V., ed. *The Norton Anthology of Short Fiction, 3rd ed.* New York, NY: W. W. Norton & Co., 1986.

Cerf, Bennett. *At Random: The Reminiscences of Bennett Cerf.* New York, NY: Random House, 1977.

Clayton, John J. *The Heath Introduction to Fiction.* Lexington, MA: D.C. Heath and Co., 1984.

Cleveland, Ceil. *Who, What, When, Where, Why in the World of Literature.* Hauppauge, NY: Barron's Educational Series, 1991.

Conn, Charis, et al. *The Complete Harper's Index.* New York, NY: Henry Holt and Co., 1991.

Craig, Hardin, and David Bevington, ed. *The Complete Works of Shakespeare, rev. ed.* Glenview, IL: Scott, Foresman & Co., 1973.

Daintith, John, et al. *The Macmillan Dictionary of Quotations.* New York, NY: Macmillan, 1989.

Davis, Norman, et al. *A Chaucer Glossary.* Oxford, UK: Oxford University Press, 1981.

Drabble, Margaret, ed. *The Oxford Companion to English Literature, 5th ed.* Oxford, UK: Oxford University Press, 1985.

Drew, Bettina. *Nelson Algren: A Life on the Wild Side.* New York, NY: G. P. Putnam's Sons, 1989.

Elliott, Emory, gen. ed. *Columbia Literary History of the United States.* New York, NY: Columbia University Press, 1988.

Ellmann, Richard. *James Joyce.* Oxford, UK: Oxford University Press, 1982.

Felton, Bruce. *Best, Worst, and Most Unusual.* New York, NY: Thomas Y. Crowell Co., 1975.

Ferris, Paul. *Dylan Thomas.* London, UK: Hodder and Stoughton, 1977.

Finneran, Richard J., ed. *The Poems of William Butler Yeats.* New York, NY: Macmillan, 1983.

Franklin, V. Benjamin, ed. *Dictionary of American Literary Characters.* New York, NY: Facts on File, 1990.

Frye, Northrop, et al. *The Harper Handbook to Literature.* New York, NY: Harper & Row, 1985.

Bibliography

Grene, David, and Richmond Lattimore, ed. *Sophocles I.* Chicago, IL: University of Chicago Press, 1954.
Grolier's Academic American Encyclopedia, Online Edition. Danbury, CT: Grolier Electronic Publishing, 1992.
Grote, David. *Common Knowledge: A Reader's Guide to Literary Allusions.* New York, NY: Greenwood Press, 1987.
Hamalian, Leo, and Edmond L. Volpe, eds. *Eleven Modern Short Novels.* New York, NY: G. P. Putnam's Sons, 1971.
Hamilton, Edith. *Mythology.* New York, NY: New American Library, 1942.
Happé, Peter, ed. *English Mystery Plays.* Harmondsworth, UK: Penguin, 1975.
Harris, Laurie Lanzen. *Characters in Twentieth Century Literature.* Detroit, MI: Gale Research, 1990.
Hart, James D. *The Oxford Companion to American Literature, 5th ed.* New York, NY: Oxford University Press, 1983.
Hartnoll, Phyllis, ed. *The Oxford Companion to the Theatre.* Oxford, UK: Oxford University Press, 1983.
Hirsch, Jr., E. D., et al. *The Dictionary of Cultural Literacy.* New York, NY: Houghton Mifflin, 1988.
Hoffman, Mark S., ed. *The World Almanac and Book of Facts.* New York, NY: Pharos Books, 1991.
Holman, C. Hugh, and William Harmon. *A Handbook to Literature.* New York, NY: Macmillan, 1986.
Hunter, J. Paul. *The Norton Introduction to Literature: Poetry.* New York, NY: Norton, 1973.
Johnson, Otto, exec. ed. *The Information Please Almanac.* Boston, MA: Houghton Mifflin, 1990.
Johnson, Samuel. *A Dictionary of the English Language.* London, UK: Times Books, 1979.
Jones, Neal T. *A Book of Days for the Literary Year.* New York, NY: Thames & Hudson, 1984.
Katz, Ephraim. *The Film Encyclopedia.* New York, NY: Perigee, 1979.
Killikelly, Sarah H. *Curious Questions in History, Literature, Art and Social Life.* Detroit, MI: Gale Research Co., 1968.
Kirkpatrick, D. L., and James Vinson. *Contemporary Novelists, 4th ed.* London, UK: St. James Press, 1986.
Kirkpatrick, D. L., ed. *Reference Guide to American Literature.* London, UK: St. James Press, 1987.
Klein, Leonard S., ed. *Encyclopedia of World Literature in the Twentieth Century.* New York, NY: Frederick Ungar, 1982.
Knight, Stephen. *Arthurian Literature and Society.* New York, NY: St. Martin's, 1983.

Lass, Abraham H., et al. *The Facts On File Dictionary of Classical, Biblical, and Literary Allusions*. New York, NY: Facts On File, 1987.

Lattimore, Richmond, trans. *Aeschylus I*. Chicago, IL: University of Chicago Press, 1953.

Levey, Judith S., and Agnes Greenhall, eds. *The Concise Columbia Encyclopedia*. New York, NY: Columbia University Press, 1983.

Lonsdale, Bernard J., and Helen K. Mackintosh. *Children Experience Literature*. New York, NY: Random House, 1973.

Macrone, Michael. *Brush Up Your Shakespeare!* New York, NY: Harper & Row, 1990.

Magill, Frank N., ed. *Cyclopedia of Literary Characters*. New York, NY: Harper & Row, 1963.

———. *Cyclopedia of Literary Characters II*. Pasadena, CA: Salem Press, 1990.

———. *Masterpieces of World Literature*. New York, NY: HarperCollins, 1989.

———. *Masterplots, rev. ed.* Englewood Cliffs, NJ: Salem Press, 1976.

———. *Masterplots II: American Fiction Series*. Englewood Cliffs, NJ: Salem Press, 1986.

———. *Masterplots II: British and Commonwealth Fiction Series*. Englewood Cliffs, NJ: Salem Press, 1987.

Manguel, Alberto, and Gianni Guadalupi. *The Dictionary of Imaginary Places*. New York, NY: Macmillan, 1980.

Moglen, Helene. *Charlotte Brontë: The Self Conceived*. New York, NY: W. W. Norton and Co., 1976.

Monaco, James. *The Encyclopedia of Film*. New York, NY: Perigee, 1991.

The New York Public Library Desk Reference. New York, NY: Prentice-Hall, 1989.

The New York Review Quiz Book. New York, NY: Crown, 1986.

The New York Times (various issues).

The New York Times Book Review (various issues).

The New Yorker (various issues).

Newsweek (various issues).

O'Connor, Flannery. *Mystery and Manners*. New York, NY: Farrar, Straus & Giroux, 1969.

O'Kill, Brian. *Exit Lines*. Burnt Mill, Harlow, Essex, UK: Longman, 1986.

O'Neill, Lois Decker, ed. *The Women's Book of World Records & Achievements*. Garden City, NY: Anchor Books, 1979.

Ousby, Ian, ed. *The Cambridge Guide to Literature in English*. Cambridge, UK: Cambridge University Press, 1988.

Parsons, Nicholas. *The Book of Literary Lists: A Collection of Anno-*

BIBLIOGRAPHY

tated Lists, Statistics, and Anecdotes Concerning Books. New York, NY: Facts On File, 1987.

Publishers Weekly (various issues).

Reader's Digest (various issues).

Rogal, Samuel J., ed. *Calendar of Literary Facts.* Detroit, MI: Gale Research, 1991.

Rood, Karen L., ed. *American Literary Almanac: From 1608 to the Present.* New York, NY: Facts On File, 1988.

Roth's American Poetry Annual. Great Neck, NY: Roth Publishing, 1989.

Salny, Abbie F. *The Mensa Book of Literary Quizzes.* New York, NY: Harper Perennial, 1991.

Seymour-Smith, Martin. *Who's Who in Twentieth Century Literature.* New York, NY: McGraw-Hill, 1976.

Steinbrenner, Chris, and Otto Penzler. *Encyclopedia of Mystery and Detection.* New York, NY: McGraw-Hill, 1976.

Stephens, Meic, ed. *A Dictionary of Literary Quotations.* London, UK: Routledge, 1990.

Sutherland, James R. *The Oxford Book of Literary Anecdotes.* Oxford, UK: Oxford University Press, 1987.

Vanity Fair (various issues).

Wallace, Amy, et al. *The Book of Lists #3.* New York, NY: Bantam, 1983.

Wallace, Irving, et al. *The Book of Lists #2.* New York, NY: Bantam, 1980.

Wallechinsky, David, et al. *The Book of Lists.* New York, NY: Bantam, 1977.

Ward, A. C., and Maurice Hussey, eds. *Longman Companion to Twentieth Century Literature, 3rd ed.* Burnt Mill, Harlow, Essex, UK: Longman, 1981.

Webster's Seventh New Collegiate Dictionary. Springfield, MA: G. & C. Merriam Co., 1969.

Weisenburger, Steven C. *A Gravity's Rainbow Companion.* Athens, GA: University of Georgia Press, 1988.

What Do You Know About Literature: Key Questions and Correct Answers. New York, NY: College Publishing Corp., 1967.

INDEX

INDEX

INDEX

INDEX

INDEX

INDEX

INDEX

INDEX

INDEX

INDEX

INDEX

INDEX